MARTIN YAN'S CHINA

MARTIN YAN'S CHINA

Photographs by Stephanie Liu Jan and Geoffrey Nilsen

CHRONICLE BOOKS
SAN FRANCISCO

Library of Congress Cataloging-in-Publication Data available.

ISBN: 978-0-8118-6396-4

Manufactured in China.

Food styling by Pouke
Design and typesetting by Idea Route
Yan Can Cook Project Manager: Tara Lee
Special thanks to Irene Yim, Julia Lee, Ivan Lai, and Elizabeth Reis

10 9 8 7 6 5 4 3 2

Chronicle Books LLC
680 Second Street
San Francisco, California 94107

www.chroniclebooks.com

HOME AGAIN

....

America is my home. Years ago, I settled down in Northern California, among the rolling hills just out-side of San Francisco. I've raised my family, run my business, and made many lifelong friends here. But I also have another home. In my heart, China is not only where I was born . . . it is a part of me that I carry wherever I travel in the world.

The China where I spent my early years was a very different place than it is today. Growing up in Guang-zhou, I was labeled a "city boy" simply because I had seen buildings as tall as . . . nine stories! These days, as I travel along the multilane highways that connect the booming industrial zones of Southern China with Guangzhou, I see buildings that are well over sixty stories tall. They stand, one next to the other, overlooking villages awakening from centuries of agrarian life. In a few short decades, China has leaped from an agrarian culture of the nineteenth century to an industrial powerhouse of the twenty-first. Spanking-new shopping malls, condos, and multiplexes rise amidst sites that mark thousands of years of Chinese history. Inside sits a new generation of Chinese, multitasking and cell-phone texting away, and quickly becoming addicted to all the trimmings of modern society. I must admit, my initial feelings about all of this were mixed. While I am proud of what China has achieved in such a short time span, I cannot help but wonder: Where did *my* China go?

There truly was a unique beauty to the simple Chinese life I recall from not so long ago. Some of my fondest childhood memories revolve around the comforting aroma in my mom's kitchen and the sound of street vendors outside as they called out their daily specials. Upon my first return to China, after years of living in North America, the first thing I looked for was a special wonton noodle street stand, one that I had been reminiscing about for years. Although it was no longer there, my disappointment was short-lived. Minutes later, down the block from my old noodle haunt, I found not one, not two, but close to a dozen food stalls. In addition to wonton noodles, one offered *dan dan* noodles, and another one the pan-fried variety. The stalls were cleaner than what I remembered, the seating was no longer cramped, and the noodles, as much as I'd like to say they were not like the old days, were just as I remembered, down to the savory broth with a hint of dried scallops.

There and then I learned a valuable lesson: Things do not have to stay the same; they can be better. Our fond memories are like comfort food. They are made up of images that warm us inside and remind us of a time when we felt nurtured and safe. I don't think we should abandon our memories. But at the same time, we should not feel devastated when things have evolved. Instead of grieving over our "losses," we can build new memories. In my many, many travels to China since my first homecoming, I've managed to build new memories upon the old ones. These images coexist, side by side, in my mind. Each one is special and real to me.

This is my eleventh book about China. In past decades, I have devoted much of my time to promoting Chinese cuisine, as well as many other Asian cuisines. From Manila to Macau, Seoul to Singapore, I have crisscrossed Asia and explored its depths, discovering an enormous wealth of diverse culinary arts. Yet inevitably I have been drawn back, time and time again, to China.

China's four established, well-recognized regional cuisines include Northern style (Mandarin), Shanghai style, Sichuan style, and Guangzhou style (Cantonese). Food critics and academics have devoted much time and effort to explaining the differences between these styles of cooking. Much ink has been devoted to explaining how climatic and cultural divergences have contributed to these distinctive styles of cooking, and to the role geography has played in determining the availability and use of particular ingredients. Regardless of the writer's perspective, the common agreement is that food in China is best defined by these four distinct geographical regions.

In my opinion, however, these categories are valid, but somewhat limiting. They derive from the notion of China as the "Middle Kingdom," dominated for four thousand years by the Han Chinese. Today, the Han descendants constitute approximately 90 percent of China's population. However, fifty-five officially recognized minority communities constitute the remaining 10 percent of the population. In a country of 1.3 billion, that 10 percent is more than 100 million people! And each community has developed its own distinctive way of cooking.

I've always been fascinated by China's minority communities. In my earlier visits to parts of Sichuan, or to the picturesque city of Guilin, I would come upon members of different ethnic groups dressed in their traditional garb. The food they presented was equally fascinating. Several of these groups are Muslim, so their diets are free of pork but rich in mutton. I tasted my first lamb skewer in the ancient city of Xian many years ago, and I was hooked!

Since then, I've been wanting to explore China's "Wild West"—the provinces of Guangxi, Guizhou, Yunnan, and Sichuan, with their minority cultures, snowcapped mountains, Tibetan monasteries, highland tea plantations, and close proximity to the ancient Silk Road. I finally got my chance. This book and this season of *Martin Yan's China* cover many different parts of China. I'm particularly excited about shining a light on the hidden "Wild West" and reaching beyond the four cuisines of China to provide my readers and viewers a more comprehensive, and perhaps more contemporary, picture of this amazing and diverse country and its food.

My journeys have been enlightening and inspiring. Time after time, I found myself amidst the most breathtaking scenes of nature. From ancient towns like Lijiang, Shuhe, and Simao, the heart of the famous Pu'er, where time has stood still for centuries, to the spectacular limestone hills that guard the banks of the Li River outside Guilin, I was awestruck by the incredible natural beauty that is a part of China's heritage. If I appear to my TV audience to be a bit distracted or tongue-tied in some of those on-location segments, that's the reason.

I found local culture, with its unusual foods, just as fascinating as the scenery. In Yunnan, out of dozens of street snacks, only eighteen were deemed unusual enough to be named the region's "odd specialties." Needless to say, I tried them all. It took the better part of two days, but it was worth the calories.

By naming this book *Martin Yan's China*, I'm not laying claim to the country. The title refers to my impressions, memories, and understanding of, and my deep-rooted feelings for, the complex and captivating country of my birth. In one of my recent trips back to Guangzhou, I was fortunate to meet up with some of my old neighbors and childhood friends, people with whom I grew up. I was amazed at how well they remembered our times together. I marveled at the different paths our respective lives have taken, and part of me will always wonder what I would be like today had I not made the journey across the Pacific all those years ago.

This past summer I brought my two boys to China for the first time. Despite all their research and language training, they weren't quite ready to face the immense scale of China, nor its fast pace. I was struck by how American my boys truly are. They looked at China from the viewpoint of two typical American teens of Chinese heritage. As much as I tried, I could not convince them to see things from my point of view: they wouldn't and couldn't. I was frustrated by this at first, but over time I realized that their memories of China should be theirs and theirs alone, just as mine are mine alone. When I gave this book the title *Martin Yan's China*, that's what I meant. These are my personal memories. I hope that passages in this book will inspire others to go and seek their own experience in China.

China is such a rich country in culture and history. I hope that my boys will build on their first impressions and that our trip was only the first of many. To them, China is not home; it's a fascinating part of the world to visit. To me, however, it is where a part of me will always reside, and every time I go back, I am going home again.

Getting
Started

In almost every interview, sooner or later, the same question usually turns up: "Chef Yan, what is your secret to good cooking?" So here it is: once and for all, my secret revealed. Every professional chef's good cooking begins with good preparation. Every award-winning chef has his or her well-stocked kitchen and pantry, with all the tools of the trade. That's where all the magic happens. Always begin with the right tools, along with the right techniques. Throw in the freshest ingredients and spices, add a dash of the chef's imagination, and there you have it: the next culinary masterpiece!

Just what makes up the must-haves and the must-knows in every Asian kitchen?
I share my list with you in this chapter.

COOKING TOOLS

Wok

This is by far the single most important and versatile cooking utensil for the Chinese cook. If I were stranded on a desert island, the three tools I would want to have are my wok, my cleaver, and my satellite phone. The wok, a concave pan, can take the place of a dozen pots and pans. Almost any type of cooking can be done in it, from stir-frying to steaming.

Woks come in a variety of sizes and styles. In the old days, they were mostly huge, were made of cast iron, and weighed 300 tons. These days, they are made from a variety of materials and they come in all sizes and designs. You can find some as small as 9 inches in diameter for home use or as large as 36 inches for restaurants. Woks can be made from spun or hand-pounded carbon steel, stainless steel, hard-anodized aluminum, and various metal alloys or layers of metal—with or without a nonstick surface. Traditional round-bottomed woks can be used with a ring stand that sits on a gas burner.

Your next question is probably, "Do I *have* to cook in a round-bottomed wok?" Athough the traditional round-bottomed wok is still the choice for many professional and Chinese home chefs, the flat-bottomed wok, a hybrid wok/frying pan, and stir-fry pans are catching up in popularity. Flat-bottomed woks are very efficient when used on home electric burners because of the increased contact with the heating element. They may have a nonstick coating. What you sacrifice in the smooth wok motion when using these woks, you gain in ease of use. Personally, I recommend having both in the kitchen. Some nights you feel like wokking; some nights you don't.

Wok ladle and spatula

Here's a tip that's seldom mentioned in most Chinese cookbooks: The round-bottomed wok doesn't work too well without a ladle and spatula. These are indispensable wok tools that were developed over almost a thousand years, along with the wok. Made from stainless steel, heat-resistant plastic, or silicon, they are designed to fit perfectly within the curving shape of the concave wok's cooking surface and can perform different functions.

Steamer

There are two common types of steamers: bamboo and metal. Designed to be stackable, steamers efficiently allow one or more dishes to be cooked simultaneously over a single wok or pot of boiling water. You can steam practically anything, from a few dumplings to a whole fish.

Though the old-fashioned bamboo steamers may burn, warp, or discolor over time, and may need to be replaced eventually, many traditional Chinese chefs still prefer them. Their woven tops allow excess steam to escape without condensing and dripping back into the food. Bamboo steamers usually come in a variety of sizes and will fit right inside a wok. For a 14-inch wok, buy a 13-inch steamer. Both metal and bamboo steamers may also be used over a regular pot of the same diameter. The only advantage to a metal steamer is longevity. Wash both kinds of steamers with hot, lightly soapy water, rinse well, dry, and store in an open shelf or cupboard.

If you don't have a steamer, or if you are marooned on the same desert island with me, you can use small cans, such as water chestnut or tuna cans, with the tops and bottoms removed as stands to hold heatproof dishes above the water in the wok. Or, simply do it the old-fashioned Chinese way and place two pairs of chopsticks in a tic-tac-toe pattern to make a stand for the heatproof dish.

Clay pot

Clay, sand, or earthenware pots make a fun and handy addition to your kitchen collection. Traditionally made just from clay and sand, they are usually found encased in a wire protective casing and come with or without covers, depending on the style. They also come in different sizes and with various methods of glazing on both the inside and the exterior. Clay pots are designed to withstand high temperatures and can be placed directly on a gas burner or in an oven. They are also great heat absorbers, which makes them perfect for braising, simmering, slow-cooking, and stewing. Here's a useful tip: you can serve in the very pot that you cook your meal in. Their earthy appearance can be attractive on dining tables. That means one fewer dish to wash after dinner.

Don't be fooled by their heaviness and sturdy appearance. Clay pots are fragile and should be handled carefully to avoid breakage. Temperature extremes are the enemy of these useful cooking vessels. Allow the pot to cool completely before immersing it in water or placing it on a damp or cold surface. Never leave a clay pot empty when placing it directly over heat. Always add liquids or ingredients first. You can find clay pots in Chinese markets and well-stocked Chinese grocery stores. Any heatproof covered casserole dish can be used as a suitable substitute.

Electric rice cooker

A common sight these days in kitchens from Sichuan to San Antonio, the electric rice cooker should never be underestimated. First of all, it makes perfect rice every time and is practically foolproof (at least for those who can follow directions). You can find models with one simple button and others with an onboard computer control panel. Their use is not limited to making rice. You can use them to make casseroles and slow-cooking dishes such as Chinese porridge. Every Asian kitchen has an electric rice cooker, and so should you.

Chinese wire strainer

The Chinese wire strainer is both unique and practical. Made with a wire mesh in the shape of a shallow ladle, with a long bamboo handle, it can be used to lift out and drain foods from either hot oil or boiling water. It is now found in most kitchenware stores and is quite inexpensive. As a substitute, use a regular slotted spoon.

Cutting boards

Found in many shapes, sizes, materials, and colors, a cutting board is the workhorse of your kitchen. A good board can save the edges of your knives so that they do not require sharpening as often. No matter what kind of board you choose (wood or plastic), it is important to sanitize it after each use, especially after cutting meat. Better yet, have one board for cutting meat and another for vegetables.

Mandoline

A French cutting tool used for slicing and cutting, mandolines can now be found in Asian markets as well. It is simply a very sharp blade mounted on a flat surface. You slide the ingredients across this surface, producing perfect cuts every time. The large French version is made from stainless steel and can be quite intimidating if you don't know how to use it. The smaller, usually plastic, Japanese version is just as useful and about a third the size and cost. It is a very useful tool that allows you to prep your vegetables in half the time, with great consistency in thickness.

Chinese cleaver

The word *cleaver* is actually a misnomer. What most people in the West commonly call a cleaver is in fact a Chinese chef's knife. A cleaver is a heavier version used for cutting through bones and meat. It has a much thicker and larger blade. The Chinese chef's knife, on the other hand, is an all-purpose cutting tool. It can be damaged if you use it to cut through bones. After a bit of practice, you can slice, dice, chop, mince, julienne, and garnish like a pro. It can also be used to transfer ingredients, to tenderize, and to smash ingredients like ginger and garlic.

There are many styles and metals to choose from. When choosing your first Chinese chef's knife, grip it in your hand and see how it feels. Once you get your knife home, keep it sharp between uses with a sharpening steel or electric knife sharpener. A sharp knife is a safe knife. Wash your knife after each use in warm, soapy water, rinse, and dry well—do not put it in the dishwasher.

TAKING CARE OF YOUR WOK: AN OWNER'S GUIDE

Proper maintenance and seasoning are the keys to successful wok cooking.

New carbon steel woks should be scoured with hot, soapy water to remove any protective coating applied at the factory.

Thoroughly dry the wok over medium heat. Towel drying alone may cause the wok to rust.

Rub a small amount of vegetable oil and ½ teaspoon of fine salt evenly into the entire cooking surface, and gently heat the wok over medium heat while occasionally rubbing the surface with a lightly oiled paper or cloth towel. If it begins to smoke, use less oil and reduce the heat slightly.

Continue this procedure until the wok begins to darken. This builds the first layer of what will become a solid "seasoned" surface and will prevent food from sticking.

The trick to maintaining and building up this layer is to wash the wok with hot water after each use. Don't use too much soap, and always dry it completely over medium heat.

Never use steel wool or abrasive pads to clean the wok. Rub in a bit of fresh oil when it is dry. The wok is then ready to use again or to be cooled and stored.

CHOOSING A HIGH-QUALITY CHINESE CHEF'S KNIFE

Choose a knife made from a stainless steel alloy that will not rust.

The metal of the blade should extend through the handle, known as a full tang. It may even be riveted.

The center of gravity is where the blade meets the handle, known as the bolster.

In twenty-first century North America, food shopping is often regarded as a chore — a necessary but unpleasant ritual that we perform once or twice a week. For someone like me, who grew up in the more rustic environment of Southern China, this is real irony. Why? Because I see food shopping in North America as an indoor leisure activity, performed in a comfy, climate-controlled environment. It's strolling down clean, well-lit aisles, where countless neat, packaged food items are stacked on shelves, beckoning for our attention. The typical Chinese farmers' market back in my younger days was noisy, hot, wet, and crowded. For me, there's really no comparison.

Chinese call their farmers' market a "Wet Market," and if you ever slosh around in one, you will understand why. Open-air markets lack refrigeration, so farmers keep splashing water on their produce to keep it fresh. Eventually, the ground gets soaked, puddles are formed, and, well, you get the picture.

Yet, as noisy, hot, and crowded as it was, a wet market was also the place where many of my best childhood memories were formed, for the market is a lively place, always full of surprises. You will find people of all ages eating at food stalls next to vegetable stands. The lack of storage space and refrigeration requires that food vendors bring in fresh supplies every day. This means you'll only find seasonal vegetables and livestock there. Fresh, organically grown foods may not always be the best looking, but they're definitely superior in taste and have great textures and wonderful nutrients. Most likely, you'll find the ducks and chickens are raised naturally and fed organically. In a typical Chinese food market, these animals usually seem smaller, not as fat or as big as animals in the West, which are fed processed foods.

Today, the reverse trend in North America is to promote sustainable farming practices and to provide people with organic, wholesome produce and free-range meats. Interestingly enough, Chinese farmers have been growing their products and producing agricultural commodities this way for thousands of years. It's still common practice in many parts of China today.

At outdoor farmers' markets in China, you will find a variety of food vendors preparing and selling delicious and unusual local favorites. It's a truly unique alfresco dining experience. Now, you will see Chinese grocery stores with a complete Chinese deli. This is also true in many Chinese cities, as well as markets in Singapore, Malaysia, Thailand, and the Philippines. In Asia, you can shop for your groceries and enjoy a delicious treat before going home. I am glad to see that this dining-in-the-food-market tradition has been exported to contemporary North America. You don't believe me? Next time you visit your air-conditioned supermarket, drop by the deli, and you may just find the local rendition of an Asian-inspired menu. Isn't progress wonderful?

COOKING TECHNIQUES

Cutting techniques

Now that you have found yourself the right Chinese chef's knife, here are some of the most common cutting techniques:

SLICING — A technique used to cut meat or vegetables into bite-sized pieces, the common dimension for Asian cooking. Hold the item firmly on the cutting board, with your fingers curled and perpendicular to the blade, and cut straight down with the knife. For an added Asian look, slice the item at a 45-degree angle. Usually the denser an item is, the longer its cooking time, so slice dense ingredients more thinly.

JULIENNE — Asian julienne is different from julienne in the West. You can simply shingle slices together and then slice through them again thinly to yield a matchstick shape. Traditional juliennes are about 2 inches long and about ⅛ inch thick.

DICING — First cut the ingredient into long sticks, and then cut across the sticks perpendicularly to make cubes of the desired size. Usually, cubing means about ¾-inch cubes. Dicing means about ¼- to ½-inch cubes, and mincing means about ¹⁄₁₆-inch cubes. Depending on who you have to impress, you may be very precise and try to get them all the same size.

CHOPPING — Cutting ingredients in an irregular dice, when consistent size is not necessary—for instance, when cutting herbs or nuts for a garnish. Cut through the item successive times and in multiple directions.

ROLL CUT — A technique used to cut long vegetables such as carrots or zucchini. First cut a diagonal slice at the tip of the vegetable. Then roll the vegetable a quarter turn and cut again at the same angle. Repeat the turning and cutting until you reach the final cut.

CHIFFONADE — This cut can be used for anything flat and flexible, such as herbs and leafy green vegetables. Stack the items to be sliced and/or roll the item up. Then slice through it thinly, to create narrow strips.

GARNISHING — There is an ancient tradition of decorating Chinese food with garnishes, both elaborate and simple. Try your hand at some simple garnishing to bring your dishes to life. It can be fun and also makes your food look as though it is fit for the emperor. There are many sources for Chinese garnishing techniques on the Internet and in countless books. Check them out and delight in the reaction of your family and friends.

Stir-frying

This quick and easy method of cooking is the most common technique used in Chinese restaurants and homes. Developed as a way to conserve resources, it is called stir-frying because the food is kept in constant motion over very high heat. By stirring or tossing to ensure even cooking, this quick, simple process retains the flavors, textures, and nutrients of the food. Below is an easy-to-follow way to prepare a stir-fry. Remember, good stir-fries don't take a long time, but they require a lot of practice.

Get ready to wok; stir-frying is very quick. Don't even blink! Make sure you have everything measured and cut up uniformly, and have marinated ingredients close at hand.

"HOT WOK, COOL OIL: FOOD WON'T STICK." First, preheat the empty wok over high heat for a couple of minutes. Place your hand over the surface and, once you can feel the heat, add the oil. Swirl the oil to coat the cooking surface, and then add the aromatics (garlic and ginger).

Not all ingredients take the same amount of cooking time. The sequence of adding ingredients is very important, to ensure that everything is cooked properly. After the aromatics, add the proteins, such as meat, seafood, or poultry. Once the meat is nearly cooked, add the vegetables. The heartier and denser ones are added before the softer and leafier ones. If they are very dense, such as carrots or large pieces of broccoli, you might want to blanch them in water or oil in advance.

"IT'S STIR-FRYING, NOT STARE-FRYING." Don't forget to stir the food around with a spatula or a pair of wooden chopsticks occasionally. High heat is what makes stir-frying fast. Keep everything moving in the wok or it'll burn. A bit of golden color is great for flavor, but if anything turns black, it will taste bitter.

Don't crowd the pan. If the wok looks like the subway at rush hour, the ingredients won't cook evenly or brown properly. To prevent this, you can cook the meats and vegetables separately: cook the meat first and remove it, and then cook the vegetables.

Most Chinese dishes call for a cornstarch mixture, to give a beautiful shine and consistency. Normally, I recommend 1 teaspoon of cornstarch dissolved in 2 teaspoons of cold water for every ¼ cup of liquid in the wok. Always mix the cornstarch with cold water or broth before adding it. Once it goes into the wok, keep stirring the liquid as it boils and thickens.

Frying

DEEP-FRYING — A frying technique that makes food crispy and golden brown. If done correctly, it does not have to be unhealthy. To deep-fry, preheat a wok or pot no more than one-third full of oil over medium-high heat until the oil reaches a temperature of 350 degrees F to no more than 375 degrees F. If it is beginning to smoke, it is too hot. If you do not have a thermometer, simply test the oil with a small amount of batter or a piece of the item to be fried. I recommend investing in an oil thermometer. It makes frying a lot safer and takes the guesswork out of it. Once the food is golden and cooked through, remove it with a wire strainer or a slotted spoon to a rack or paper towels to drain or absorb excess oil.

SHALLOW-FRYING — This type of frying takes place in a skillet or wok with just enough oil for an item to float in. The food can be flipped and rotated as necessary. This technique works great for things that are breaded and flat. Preheat a wok or skillet with a small amount of oil. Once the oil is hot but not smoking, gently add a small amount of the item to the pan (sliding it in so it lands away from you). Fry on both sides until crispy, golden, and cooked through. Work in batches until everything is golden and delicious.

Marinating

There are many ways to add flavor to your meat and vegetables, both before and after cooking. Marinating is simply a process by which you allow the meat or vegetables to mingle with your desired flavors before cooking. Once the food is cooked, the outside is delicious and the inside moist and flavorful. The main ingredient in most marinating is salt or soy sauce. Salt allows the flavor to go into the actual cells of the muscle or plant; meanwhile it pulls out water, concentrating the flavor.

Dry-rubbing

Used exclusively for meat, dry-rubbing is the same as marinating, but it usually contains a lot more spices and less moisture. It makes an intense crust and seals in the juices for cooking methods like roasting and smoking.

Brining

You can brine any kind of meat. Simply add an equal amount of salt and sugar, plus any other spices, tea, or herbs you wish to flavor the meat with, to warm water (about a half cup of each ingredient per quart of water). Allow the mixture to cool, then add the meat and let it stand, covered and refrigerated, for one day per pound of meat. If the pieces are small, a couple of hours should be enough.

Pickling

Just like brining except with half the salt and with some kind of vinegar added, pickling involves cooking or salting, rinsing the item to make it absorbent, adding a salty, sweet-and-sour liquid to it, and letting it stand, refrigerated, until the item has absorbed the flavors. You can pickle just about anything. It is used as a form of preservation all over the world.

Blanching

IN OIL — Blanching in oil can be used for any meat, and it also works great for vegetables such as green beans and eggplant. For vegetables, it locks in the beautiful color while cooking them to a perfect tender-crisp texture. With meat, it locks in the moisture and gives it an unbelievably soft texture—so soft that we call the process "velveting." The standard temperatures are lower than in frying, ranging from 280 degrees F to 300 degrees F. Otherwise, this process is exactly like deep-frying.

IN WATER — This technique is commonly used to quickly precook vegetables in boiling water. Bring a wok or large pot of water to a boil. Add the vegetables and cook for a few minutes, until crisp-tender or until the color turns bright. Quickly remove the vegetables from the wok and rinse under cool water to stop the cooking process. Blanching should also be used to remove the metallic taste from canned vegetables such as bamboo shoots or straw mushrooms.

Toasting

Used to release the flavor of ingredients such as nuts, seeds, and whole spices. Place the ingredients in a small, dry pan and cook over low heat, shaking the pan frequently, until slightly darkened and fragrant. Small amounts of nuts can be toasted using this technique; however, larger amounts should be toasted on a baking sheet in a 350 degree F oven until golden brown.

Roasting

In China, roasting has generally been done in restaurants, since most homes do not have ovens. In traditional Chinese ovens, marinated meats or poultry hang on hooks and cook over a wood-burning fire. This technique allows the air to circulate, resulting in a crisp exterior and a tender, moist interior. To duplicate this method in a home oven, place the marinated meat on a rack in a foil-lined baking sheet. Baste the meat with the marinade, pan juices, or a lightly sweet solution, and turn occasionally to allow even roasting.

Wok-smoking

Much faster than Western-style smoking, classic Chinese wok-smoking originated in the Sichuan region because of a special type of aromatic wood, called camphor, that is native to the area. Sometimes it is called tea-smoking because tea and other dry aromatics can be added to the wood for additional flavor. Simply line two woks with several layers of foil, allowing the excess to hang over the side. Place wood chips and aromatics into one wok and place a rack a few inches above them. Place the item to be smoked onto the rack. Cover with the other wok, roll up the foil to create a tight seal, and cook over high heat until the wok is filled with smoke. Let it sit and cool to allow the smoke to settle onto the food. Always wok-smoke in a well-ventilated area and with your stove fan on high.

Steaming

One of the best ways to retain the natural flavor and nutritional value of your ingredients. Steaming is also a very healthy cooking technique because it uses little or no fats or oils.

To steam, bring water to a boil in a wok or wide frying pan. Place the food in a heatproof dish and place it on a steamer rack above boiling water. (See the discussion of bamboo steamers on page 15 for details regarding steamers.) Cover the steamer with a tight-fitting lid and steam until the food is done, adding additional water as needed. Remember to be very careful when removing the steamer lid. Always tilt the lid away from yourself, so the escaping steam will not burn you.

Braising

This technique is commonly used to cook bigger, tougher cuts of meat, which require a longer cooking time. However, in Asian cooking, braising is also used to cook bite-sized pieces. Braising is a two-step process. First, brown the meat lightly to seal in the juices and give it a nice color. Then add liquid and seasonings one-third to one-half of the way up the side of the meat. Cover the wok or pan and place it on the stove top to cook over low heat for a few hours. In some instances, cooking time will be shorter. The meat will be very tender and succulent as a result of the long cooking time.

Stewing

Much like braising, stewing involves covering the ingredients completely with liquid. The final consistency should be thicker than that of a soup, but a stew will have larger pieces of vegetable and meat than a soup. The cooking time is also similar to braising: anywhere from a few hours to 15 minutes, depending on the ingredients used.

Red cooking

A technique in which foods gently simmer over low heat in a liquid consisting mainly of soy sauce and sugar. The food takes on a deep mahogany-colored glaze. Red-cooked meats come out tender and juicy, with a rich, full-bodied flavor from the sauce.

Confit

A traditional French process of preservation, commonly used before refrigeration was invented. Fruit confit involves preserving fruit in a sugar and water solution and then allowing it to dry. Meat confit, usually duck legs, is cured with salt and aromatics and then cooked in its own fat until the meat is nearly falling off the bone. It is then cooled and stored in its own cooking fat. Both types of confits will last at room temperature for a week or longer. Under refrigeration, the confits will last at least a month.

GLOSSARY OF INGREDIENTS

For seasoned home cooks and weekend "kitchen warriors" with a fine Asian repertoire, most of the Asian ingredients listed in the recipe sections of this book will be old friends. To others, however, they may sound a bit exotic. Don't worry; with a bit of practice, these ingredients will become lifelong companions.

BAMBOO SHOOTS — These come fresh, canned, or in vacuum-sealed bags. Tender and crisp, bamboo shoots have a naturally sweet flavor. They can be shredded or sliced. When they are young and tender, they are the perfect textural addition to stir-fries and soups.

BEAN THREAD NOODLES — Semitransparent bean thread noodles are made from mung bean starch. They look like bunches of stiff nylon fishing line. Also called cellophane or glass noodles, they come in a number of different lengths and thicknesses, depending on their country of origin. Their delicate, mild flavor is perfect in soups. Deep-fry dried noodles a small handful at a time and watch them puff and expand. Use deep-fried noodles to garnish salads and many other dishes. Bean thread noodles are sold in 1-pound or 2-ounce packages. Store opened packages in a tightly sealed container in a cool, dry place.

BLACK BEAN GARLIC SAUCE — This is simply a prepared sauce made from Chinese fermented black beans, garlic, and other seasonings. It adds a rich, salty flavor to stir-fries and steamed dishes. It is also at home with vegetables, meats, and seafood. Store opened sauce for up to a year in the refrigerator.

BLACK MUSHROOMS — Both Chinese black mushrooms and their Japanese cousins, shiitakes, have tough stems that are usually not eaten. Black mushrooms are available fresh or dried. The cap is dark brown, rich and meaty, and it has light brown gills. Dried black mushrooms are often sealed in plastic packages and can be found in Asian markets. Store dried mushrooms in a tightly sealed container in a cool, dry place, and they will keep for several months. Store fresh mushrooms in a brown paper bag in the refrigerator; they will last for about a week.

CARDAMOM — Available in black and green-colored seed pods, cardamom adds an unmistakable fragrance and flavor to the dishes of South Asia and northern Europe. You may also find the seeds ground or removed from the pod. In China, the smoky-flavored black cardamom is the main type used for soups, stews, and sweet beverages.

CHILI BEAN PASTE —This reddish-brown paste is made from fermented soybeans, fermented fava beans, or a mixture of both (depending on the brand). Generally, the darker the paste, the more "mature" it is, giving it a saltier and spicier flavor. As with most fermented soybean products, it has a salty, beanlike flavor and somewhat thick consistency. Use whole and ground bean sauces and pastes interchangeably. Chili bean paste is available in cans and jars and will keep for several months when well covered in the refrigerator.

CHILI GARLIC SAUCE — Made from a blend of fresh and dried chiles and vinegar, this salty and spicy sauce contains garlic, ginger, soybeans, and sesame oil. Every country and some regions of Asia have their own version of this sauce. Choose the one that has the best balance of spiciness and chili flavor for your taste buds. One of my favorites is made by the Lee Kum Kee sauce company.

CHILI OIL — This hot reddish-orange oil is made by infusing whole dried red chiles or crushed red pepper flakes into heated oil. Paprika adds to the reddish color. Keep chili oil on the shelf for up to a year. Use sparingly because the spiciness can easily be overwhelming.

CHINESE ALMONDS — Much smaller than regular almonds, Chinese almonds are actually a type of apricot kernel. Used often in medicinal dishes as well as many popular sweet or savory dishes, Chinese almonds come in both bitter and mildly sweet forms.

CHINESE BLACK VINEGAR — Called Chinkiang vinegar or sweet black vinegar, this is quite similar to Italy's balsamic vinegar. The mixture is a result of fermenting rice, wheat, millet, or sorghum. It is commonly used to add a dark, deep color and a sweet-sour flavor to dishes, specifically those from the eastern regions of China. It can also be used as a table condiment for dumplings.

CHINESE CHIVES — Unlike the conventional Western chives, the Chinese variety has a distinct garlic flavor and aroma. They're also beautiful, like large blades of grass, which makes them a perfect garnish. Yellow garlic chives have shorter, more tender leaves and a mild onion-garlic flavor. Flowering garlic chives have firm stalks with small, edible flower buds at the top. Look for buds that have not yet opened; they're younger and more tender. Use them quickly because they do not stay fresh for more than a few days.

CHINESE EGG NOODLES — Sold both fresh and dried, these noodles are made from wheat flour, eggs, and water, and they come in a large variety of thicknesses. They also come in shrimp and chicken flavors. You can find them in many supermarkets and a much larger selection in Asian markets. Keep fresh noodles in the freezer for up to six months or in the refrigerator for up to a week.

CHINESE FIVE-SPICE POWDER — In ancient China, the number five was believed to have curative powers. Modern Chinese five-spice powder may actually contain a few more than five ingredients. Common five-spice includes cinnamon, star anise, fennel, clove, ginger, licorice, Sichuan peppercorn, and dried tangerine peel. Use it to flavor braised meats, roasts, and barbecues. Store it in a jar with a tight lid in a cool, dry place for up to a year.

CHINESE LONG BEANS — Also called yard-long beans, Chinese long beans are quite similar to regular green beans. They are a bit firmer and more fibrous and can grow up to three feet long. Use them as you would conventional green beans. The texture can be greatly accentuated by oil-blanching. Look for firm, long, bright green beans in bunches. Store unused beans in the vegetable crisper for no more than a week.

CHINESE OKRA — Similar in flavor to zucchini, Chinese okra is also known as angled loofah. It has lengthwise ridges along its long, tapered exterior. Chinese okra bears no relation to the okra used in India, Africa, and the southern United States. It should be trimmed before cooking and is delicious in stir-fries and steamed dishes.

CHINESE RED DATES — Preserved and dried red dates, or jujubes, resemble large, wrinkled red raisins. They have a sweet and tart, almost applelike, flavor. They are used in many sweet and medicinal applications. Red dates are not a snack food.

CHINESE RICE WINE — Fermented from glutinous rice and water, this wine is not at all like wine made from grapes. The most world-renowned Chinese rice wine is the amber-gold-colored Shaoxing, named after a region near Shanghai. This smooth, nutty wine resembles dry sherry and is an essential flavoring ingredient in authentic Chinese cuisine. Do not confuse it with ordinary cooking rice wine, which contains salt.

CHINESE SAUSAGE — These mildly sweet dry-cured links are made from duck, pork, and/or beef. They have a deep red to brown color and a bumpy texture. They can be used in any dish you would use regular sausage in. Chinese sausage is shelf-stable and doesn't require refrigeration, but it will retain its flavor longer when refrigerated.

CHRYSANTHEMUM TEA — Yellow or white chrysanthemum flowers are boiled and steeped like tea to make a sweet drink in many parts of Asia. The resulting beverage is known simply as chrysanthemum tea. It has many medicinal uses, such as helping in recovery from influenza.

CILANTRO — Also known as Chinese parsley or fresh coriander, cilantro has flat, ruffled leaves and a distinct aromatic flavor. The seed, known as coriander, is also used as a spice throughout the world. Many consider cilantro to be an acquired taste. Use it with discretion and mainly as a garnish so that you can remove it easily. Fresh cilantro will keep for at least a week. It's best wrapped in a damp paper towel and kept in the refrigerator.

CONDENSED MILK — Condensed milk is simply evaporated milk with sugar added to thicken and sweeten it. It can be used in savory dishes, desserts, and baked goods to add a concentrated and sweet milky flavor. I like it in my coffee, on the rare occasion that I am not drinking tea.

CRYSTALLIZED GINGER — Crystallized ginger is made by slowly simmering fresh ginger in sugar syrup and then rolling it in granulated sugar and allowing it to dehydrate. The process brings out ginger's mellow but spicy sweet taste.

CURRY POWDER—A complex mixture of ground dry spices that varies widely from region to region, Chinese-style curry powder, used mainly in Southern China, is usually yellow and milder than most Indian or Thai curries.

DAIKON—A white to pale-green radish with a crisp and mildly spicy flavor, daikon can range from eight to fourteen inches in length and can be used in salads, stir-fries, and soups. It will keep for more than a week in the refrigerator. Daikon should be used while fresh and crisp; once it starts to get limp, it can be used as a garnish.

DUMPLING WRAPPERS—Most wrappers we find in the market are made with egg noodle dough (flour, water, and a small amount of egg). They differ mainly in shape and thickness. Wonton and egg roll wrappers are square, while pot-sticker wrappers, also sold as Japanese gyoza wrappers, are round. The thicker skins are for dumplings that will be deep-fried, pan-fried, and steamed, and the thinner ones are for dumplings that will be simmered in soup.

ENOKI MUSHROOMS—These tiny white mushrooms have small caps and long, slender stems. They have a mild and lightly sweet flavor that is great for clear soups or in raw salads. They also make an attractive sushi garnish. Look for them shrink-wrapped in the produce section.

EGGPLANT—There are many varieties of eggplants from Asia. Chinese eggplants fall in the purple to lavender color spectrum and range from three to nine inches in length. In general, Asian eggplants are sweet and relatively seedless, unlike their Italian cousins. They are best used the day of purchase, but can be wrapped in plastic wrap and kept refrigerated for several days.

FERMENTED BEAN PASTE—Similar to a seasoned Japanese miso paste, this Chinese predecessor is mildly sweet, savory, and sometimes contains chili paste. In Sichuan Province, it is added to give a well-rounded savory, almost meaty flavor to vegetable dishes. It is also used as a condiment to flavor stir-fries, stews, and soups. The color of the paste ranges from light tan to reddish brown and dark brown. It is also called ground or sweet bean sauce.

FERMENTED BLACK BEANS—These salted, fermented, and dried black beans have a pungent, earthy flavor. After they are quickly rinsed and lightly crushed, they can be used in many different dishes. They will keep for up to a year when tightly sealed and stored in a cool, dry place.

FISH SAUCE—A thin, salty, amber-colored, pungent seasoning agent, fish sauce is as popular in Southeast Asia and Southern China as soy sauce. The distinctive aroma of fermented fish mellows with cooking and adds a delicious, slightly salty taste to stews, marinades, and dipping sauces. Store fish sauce in a cool, dry place for several months.

GARLIC—Used throughout Asia and Europe, garlic is an indispensable aspect of many of the world's best-known cuisines. It is also used for medicinal purposes. In China, garlic is used as an aromatic in nearly every kind of dish. Fresh garlic keeps in its papery skin for several weeks in a cool, dry place. You may refrigerate peeled or prechopped garlic for several days.

GINKGO NUTS—Ginkgo nuts are known to possess properties that will help strengthen the intellect. Call it brain food in a hard shell. You can buy these small, oval nuts shelled and canned, vacuum sealed in their boiled form, or dried whole and raw in the shell. Use ginkgo nuts in soups, rice stuffing, and stews.

GINSENG—Ginseng is one of Asia's most prized medicinal ingredients. People pay hundreds of dollars per pound for ginseng roots from China, Japan, Korea, Siberia, and the United States. Because of its unique humanlike shape, many Asians believe that ginseng root is a cure-all. It is available in whole and cut dried forms and as a powder to flavor teas. Store ginseng root and tea in separate, tightly sealed containers and keep them in a cool, dry place for up to several months.

GREEN CHILES—Green chiles are used fresh and are available in varieties too numerous to mention. Like red chiles, their spiciness depends greatly on the variety, but green chiles are unripe and have a more green, bitter flavor. Common varieties are the jalapeño and serrano. The Anaheim variety is available canned. All chiles originated in the Americas.

GROUND GINGER—Ground and fresh ginger taste quite different, and ground ginger is a poor substitute for fresh. When substituting fresh ginger for ground ginger, do so at a ratio of 6 parts fresh for 1 part ground. Ground ginger is best when you are looking for the hotter flavor components of ginger root.

HOISIN SAUCE—Made from a mixture of fermented soybean paste, plum sauce, sweet potato purée, vinegar, garlic, sugar, and spices, this thick sauce has a sweet-spicy flavor and a reddish-brown color. It is perfect for everything from stir-fries to barbecues. Hoisin sauce also works as a table condiment for soups, stews, mushu, Peking duck, Chinese pancakes, and steamed buns. It is available in bottles and jars. Refrigerate for up to a year once opened.

JICAMA—Commonplace in Latin America, jicama (pronounced "HEE ka ma") resembles a large turnip with a brown, papery skin. Its crunchy white flesh and slightly sweet flavor make it a perfect substitute for fresh water chestnuts. Peel and use it in salads, stews, and stir-fried dishes. It can also be steamed, braised, or deep-fried.

LEEKS—The leek is related to onion and garlic. The edible portions are the white base and the light green stalk. The tender core can be eaten, but as leeks age, the core becomes woody and generally unusable. Fresh leeks can be stored in your refrigerator for up to a week.

LEMONGRASS—With an aromatic scent and subtle lemony flavor, lemongrass resembles a grasslike, woody stalk with coarse leaves. It has a yellow-green exterior and, when fresh and young, a beautiful purple interior. Infuse it in teas, grind it into pastes for curries, toss large chunks into soups, and mince and sprinkle the tender heart of it into stir-fries and salads. Fresh lemongrass can last a couple of weeks in the vegetable crisper.

LI HING MUI POWDER—Also known as crack seed or *see mui, li hing mui* powder is a dehydrated extract of plum with sugar and salt. It is used as a seasoning agent for many kinds of sweets and dehydrated or preserved fruits.

LYCHEES—Fresh lychees go from light green to pink to dark red as they ripen. They have bumpy leathery skin, semitranslucent flesh, and a single shiny, smooth, mahogany-colored seed. Both canned and fresh lychees can be sugary sweet, with a taste and texture similar to those of soft grapes. Pick bunches that are heavy, with bright, unblemished skins. They will keep in the refrigerator for up to several weeks. Transfer the contents of an unopened can to a tightly sealed container and refrigerate for up to several days.

MINT—A cool, refreshing, and very common herb, mint is used to flavor many dishes, drinks, and desserts throughout the world. Roll it up in some damp paper towels to increase its life in the refrigerator.

MUSTARD POWDER—This is finely ground mustard seed used in sauces, as a seasoning, and in salad dressings. Available in Western and Asian markets, the Chinese version is quite a bit stronger than the American yellow mustard and has a clean-tasting hotness comparable to Dijon. Powdered mustard can be stored for up to 6 months in a dry, dark place.

NAPA CABBAGE—Either short and oblong or tall and slender, napa cabbage has a sweet, creamy white stalk and frayed, ruffled, pale green to yellow edges. Use it as you would regular cabbage, but keep in mind that the napa variety is much more tender. Do not overcook it; about 2 to 5 minutes is enough. It will keep in the refrigerator for at least a week.

OOLONG TEA—*Oolong* is a Chinese colloquial term that means "making a mistake." Legends had it that oolong tea was originally an accidental mixture. Today the term *oolong* simply refers to a tea that has been semioxidized and fermented. Its flavor falls in between green tea and black tea. There are many different varieties of oolong from mainland China and Taiwan; some are even "watered" with milk during the last month of the growing cycle. Loose-leaf tea (as opposed to teabags) tends to be higher quality and is better suited for drinking and cooking.

OYSTER-FLAVORED SAUCE—A dark brown, thick, glossy, all-purpose seasoning agent made from oyster extracts, sugar, seasonings, and cornstarch. It has a distinct sweet-smoky taste that goes well with practically any meat and vegetable combination, as an ingredient or as a table condiment. Oyster-flavored sauce is also available in spicy and vegetarian styles. A refrigerated bottle of oyster-flavored sauce will keep for at least a year.

PANKO—The Japanese breadcrumbs known as panko give a whole new dimension of golden crispness to fried foods. They are larger than regular breadcrumbs and therefore retain their crispness, even after frying. Panko will go stale within a few months, but since it is so versatile—you can even use it in meat loaf or as a topping for baked macaroni and cheese—it usually gets used up quickly.

PLUM SAUCE—A mixture of salted plums, apricots, yams, rice vinegar, chiles, sugars, and other spices, this very versatile bottled sauce has a sweet, tangy, mildly fruity, and salty taste. Serve it with any crispy dish or with roasted meats, or add it to salad dressings or dips. Once opened, store plum sauce in the refrigerator for up to a year.

POMELO—A very large, pear-shaped, yellow-skinned relative of the grapefruit, pomelo is also known as a Chinese grapefruit. It is particularly popular during festivals as a symbol of good fortune. Pomelo has a thick, fragrant peel and a sweet, dry pulp that is very different from that of other citrus fruits. The fruits are available from January to March. Choose fruits that are fragrant and heavy. Refrigerate ripe pomelos for up to a week; let the unripe ones sit on the counter until slightly softened.

PORK SUNG—This dried, shredded Chinese pork product has a light, fluffy texture similar to that of coarse cotton. It is used as a topping for many foods, such as rice porridge, tofu, and savory soymilk. It is also used as a filling for various buns and pastries and as a snack food on its own.

RED BEAN PASTE—Red bean paste or adzuki bean paste is a sweet, dark paste that originated in China. It is used in Chinese sweet dishes and in soups. The beans are boiled, mashed, strained into a fine paste, and sweetened with sugar or honey.

RED CHILES—Available both dried and fresh, red chiles are originally from the Americas. Europeans brought them to Asia in the mid-1600s. A red chile is fully ripe, and its spiciness varies greatly, depending on the variety. In China, red chiles are used mainly in dried form, both whole and crushed, in the fiery dishes of the western provinces.

RED FERMENTED BEAN CURD—Fermented bean curd is a soft, creamy curd with a smooth, thick, custardlike texture. It has a subtle spiciness and a distinctive fermented flavor. In Southern China, it serves as a common table condiment and as a seasoning for leafy green vegetables. Once opened, it will keep for several months in the refrigerator.

RICE—No other grain is as important to Asia as rice. It can be steamed, boiled, baked in casseroles, or used to make noodles and dumpling wrappers. The common varieties of rice are long, medium, and short grain; fragrant basmati and jasmine; and sticky Chinese and Southeast Asian glutinous or sweet rice. Most varieties can be found brown, with the bran layer intact, or highly polished and white. All types of rice have different preferred cooking methods, water amounts, and cooking times. For the best results in this book, follow the recommended cooking time in each recipe.

RICE NOODLES—*Hor fun,* or fresh rice noodles, are made from long-grain rice flour and water. They are soft, pliable, milky white noodles that are found in whole folded sheets, wide-cut strips, or as thin spaghetti-like strands in the refrigerated section of Asian markets. Choose noodles that are soft and spongy to the touch. Although fresh rice noodles are best on the day of purchase, they can be stored in the refrigerator for several days. The noodles will be stiff after refrigeration; rinse them gently with boiling water before cooking to soften them and remove the oily coating.

RICE VINEGAR—Made from fermented rice, this Japanese product has a milder and sweeter flavor than distilled white vinegar. It is used to make sweet-and-sour dishes and salad dressings, and to season vegetables or stir-fries.

ROCK SUGAR—Rock sugar, or rock candy, looks like a large, pale amber-colored crystal, made from a combination of refined and unrefined sugars and honey. This type of sugar adds a smooth, refreshing sweetness to foods. A one-inch piece is about the same as one-and-a-half tablespoons of white sugar. Rock sugar is available in plastic packages and in cellophane-wrapped boxes and will keep for several months.

SESAME OIL—Aromatic and uniquely strong-flavored, sesame oil is either golden or dark brown. It is made from roasted white sesame seeds and is used primarily as a flavoring agent in marinades. Small amounts are added toward the end of cooking for a final aromatic seasoning. It can keep for a long time when refrigerated, although it may solidify under extreme cold.

SESAME SEEDS—White sesame seeds, hulled or unhulled, have a sweet, nutty flavor. Black sesame seeds are mildly bitter. Only white sesame seeds need to be toasted before using to intensify their flavor and aromatic fragrance. Both white and black seeds are available in larger quantities and at much lower prices in Asian markets. Store them in a tightly sealed plastic bag, and refrigerate. They will keep for up to several months.

SHALLOTS—A member of the onion family, shallots have a mild, sweet flavor that is subtler than onion and less aromatic than garlic. Popular in classic European cuisine, shallots are also used as an ingredient and garnish in many Southeast Asian dishes. Store as you would onions or garlic.

SHANGHAI BABY BOK CHOY—A smaller variety of bok choy, Shanghai baby bok choy has dark to light-green leaves and stalks and bright yellow flowers when in bloom. It's probably the most common vegetable in Shanghai, where it's simply called "green vegetable." It can be kept fresh in the vegetable crisper for up to a week.

SICHUAN PEPPERCORNS—Despite their name, Sichuan peppercorns are not related to common black pepper-corns. Although they resemble reddish brown seeds, they are actually dried berries. Leaving a pleasantly numbing after-taste, they are used in many signature dishes from Western China. Ground Sichuan peppercorn is one of the main ingredients in Chinese five-spice powder. It is sometimes labeled as red or wild pepper. Store Sichuan peppercorns in a jar with a tight-fitting lid, and keep them in a cool, dry place. They will keep for several months.

SICHUAN PRESERVED VEGETABLES—Various leafy green vegetables such as mustard greens, napa cabbage, and bok choy are preserved with salt, vinegar, and spices before being sealed in cans, earthenware, glass jars, or, at times, in travel-sized vacuum foil packages. They are used as ingredients or garnishes in soups, stews, rice porridge, and stir-fries.

SMITHFIELD HAM—Not all hams are created equal. Look for Smithfield when the recipe calls for it. Its dark red color, salty taste, and chewy texture are indispensable in a variety of dishes. It is also labeled "Virginia ham" in some markets. It is made by rubbing the ham with salt and allowing it to cure in a cool, dry place.

SOY SAUCE—Originally from China, soy sauce is now found all over the world. It is made from naturally fermented soybeans, wheat, and water. Use it to marinate, stir-fry, braise, roast, or glaze, and for nearly any seasoning application. Chinese soy sauce can be dark, thick, and sweet, or thin, light, and salty. Indonesian-style soy sauce can be very thick and sweet. Japan produces a wide variety of soy sauces, from reduced-sodium, mushroom-flavored, or wheat- and gluten-free to the moderate sweet-salty style.

SPRING ROLL WRAPPERS—Made of wheat flour and water, spring roll wrappers can be square or round. They are thinner than egg roll wrappers. Store the wrappers in a tightly sealed plastic bag in the refrigerator for up to a week, or freeze them for up to several months. Defrost frozen wrappers in the bag to retain their moisture. When working with the wrappers, take out only a few at a time and cover the rest with a damp cloth to prevent them from drying.

STAR ANISE—No other spice in the world looks like star anise. Each one-inch star has eight points, and each point contains a shiny, mahogany-colored seed. Star anise has a spiced licorice flavor that complements both meats and poultry in red-cooked or barbecued dishes and in rich braising sauces or stews. Ground star anise is used to make Chinese five-spice powder and other flavorful powders and dipping sauces. Keep star anise in a jar with a tight-fitting lid and store it in a cool, dry place.

STRAW MUSHROOMS—With a delicate sweetness and a firm, meaty texture, straw mushrooms have a brown, dome-shaped cap and a thick, straw-colored stem. Before using straw mushrooms, drain and rinse them under tap water to remove any trace of the salty canning liquid. If the mushrooms have a metallic taste, blanch them in boiling water. Store mushrooms in the refrigerator, in a tightly sealed plastic container filled with water. They will keep for a week.

SUGARCANE—Crystallized sugar was reportedly used 2,500 years ago in India. Around the eighth century A.D., Arabs introduced sugar to the Mediterranean, and it was cultivated in Spain. It was among the earliest crops brought to the Americas by Spaniards. Street vendors offer fresh sugarcane juice in many parts of south Asia and Latin America. It is used to make refined sugar and also actual sticks of fresh and canned sugarcane, which are used for culinary purposes throughout Southeast Asia.

SUGAR SNAP PEAS—Chubby cousins of the snow pea, sugar snap peas have a sweet flavor and crunchy texture when fresh. Be sure to cook them only until tender-crisp. They can be blanched briefly in water or hot oil and used in hot dishes, or eaten raw in salads. Keep them chilled and they will stay fresh for a few days.

SWEET CHILI SAUCE—Traditionally used as a table condiment, sweet chili sauce is made from ground red chiles, sugar, garlic, and salt. This thick sauce is a wonderful combination of sweet, spicy, and tangy flavors. It can be used as a glaze or added to other sauces to deliver a spicy punch.

TANGERINE PEEL—Dried tangerine peel, when reconstituted, can be added whole to stir-fries, soups, teas, and dumpling fillings to add a light, earthy, citrus flavor. Chinese herbalists use it to relieve coughing, hiccups, and nausea. The underside of the peel is bitter. Remove the white part to reduce the bitterness. Store dry peels in an airtight container for up to a year.

TOFU—I love tofu's ability to adopt the flavor of whatever sauce or ingredients it's served with. This versatile food agrees with almost any cooking method. Chinese chefs steam, chill, braise, stir-fry, and deep-fry it. Tofu is sold in a huge variety of textures and packages. Keep any unused portion in the refrigerator and use within a week for maximum freshness.

UNSWEETENED COCONUT MILK—Not to be confused with coconut juice, this is the unsweetened liquid pressed from freshly grated mature coconut meat after it has been boiled in water. The liquid has a delicious nutty creaminess, and it adds a mild, sweet, rich flavor to dishes from Southern China and Southeast Asia. It is sold in cans. Unused coconut milk can be stored for up to a week in the refrigerator.

VEGETABLE OIL—Made from a combination of vegetable seeds like corn, canola, safflower, and sunflower, vegetable oil is preferred in Chinese cooking for its high heat tolerance. It can get hotter in a wok without reaching its smoke point. It has replaced peanut oil for deep-frying because so many people these days are allergic to peanuts.

WATER CHESTNUTS—Fresh water chestnuts are pointy-topped, shiny brown, round tubers. Inside, they are a bright white color, and they have a sweet, slightly starchy taste. Fresh water chestnuts may be harder to find, but they are worth the search. Canned water chestnuts are fine as a substitute. You should blanch the canned variety to remove the "tinny" taste. Choose fresh water chestnuts that are wrinkle-free, and store them, refrigerated, in a paper bag for up to a week. Peeled and frozen, they can last for up to a month. Do not use if they are moldy or dark yellow on the inside.

WOOD EAR MUSHROOMS—This edible but very bland shelf fungus grows on trees. It is used not for flavor but for its crunchy texture and dark color. Like all dried mushrooms, wood ear mushrooms must be soaked, rinsed, and trimmed of any hard, woody parts. Use thinly sliced in soups and stir-fries.

WOLFBERRIES—Called *goji* by native Chinese, wolfberries have a long tradition in folk medicine. Ancient Chinese medicines utilize wolfberries for strengthening the eyes, liver, and kidneys as well as fortifying the *qi* (chi), or life force. They are usually sold in small packages in Asian markets and added to garnish savory and sweet soups and braises.

XO SAUCE—XO sauce is a spicy, flavorful sauce made from dried scallops, dried shrimp, garlic, and chili. Due to the exotic nature of its ingredients, XO sauce can be quite expensive. It is used to enhance the flavor of meat, seafood, tofu, and vegetable dishes. It is also served as a table condiment. Once opened, it can be kept in the refrigerator for up to a year.

THE CHINESE PANTRY

My kitchen is my office, and my pantry is my office supplies cabinet! A well-stocked pantry is the starting point of many of my best-planned menus. A tip to all home cooks: A well-organized pantry will save you time and effort in every meal. Since I don't believe in waste—be it money or precious pantry space—I am listing only the absolute pantry essentials below. Ambitious readers are always encouraged to add to these basics. Also, I would recommend replenishing your supplies well before the last jar or can of anything is used up. I generally buy more than one of each at a time at my favorite Asian grocery store. These are nonperishables, so they will keep for a fairly long time. To run out of a crucial ingredient at the last minute can be frustrating, and limiting to your menu planning.

SAUCES
Soy sauce: regular, light, and dark
Chili garlic sauce
Oyster-flavored sauce
Hoisin sauce

RICE & NOODLES
Rice: long grain
Noodles: fresh and dried

BASIC FLAVORING/SPICES
Rock sugar
Cornstarch
Red chile flakes
White pepper
Chinese five-spice powder
Curry powder
Star anise

OIL, VINEGAR & COOKING WINE
Rice wine
Black vinegar
Rice vinegar
Vegetable oil
Sesame oil

SEEDS, DRIED VEGETABLES, CANNED VEGETABLES & OTHER CANNED GOODS
Bamboo shoots
Dried shiitake (or Chinese black) mushrooms
Sesame seeds
Coconut milk
Chicken broth
Salted black beans

Basics

Here's a question at the top of every home cook's list: How can I obtain quality, maintain consistency, and serve dinner in less than thirty minutes? One quick answer has been: use bottled and prepackaged sauces. This is not necessarily a bad thing; they sure save a lot of time and energy. However, because different brands vary greatly in their ingredients and flavoring profile, what you gain in speed you might lose in quality and flavor.

So what's the solution? The answer came to me years ago when I toured the kitchens of some of the best Chinese restaurants. Instead of using bottled and premixed sauces, the chefs mixed and prepared all their common sauces on-site and from scratch. Because the sauces are made from fresh ingredients, the quality and taste are never compromised. Since then, I've been advocating that same approach to home cooks everywhere.

Having premixed sauces and broth handy will not only speed up your cooking time, it will also allow you to expand your culinary horizon. For instance, if you know how to make Sichuan Kung Pao Sauce (page 47), you can stir-fry your favorite protein with it, experiment with a new protein choice, or try the sauce on different vegetables. And with today's advanced food technology, you can easily premake and freeze the Rich Homemade Broth (page 49) for up to six months and make literally hundreds of different soups with it. Take a bit of time on a weekend to make some of these basic sauces, flavored oils, dressings, and side dishes. It's a fun project that will pay dividends down the road. You won't regret it. You'll save lots of time on your hectic weeknights and treat your family and yourself to food of consistent quality and taste.

All-Purpose Stir-Fry Sauce

Since stir-frying is one of the most popular Chinese cooking techniques, it makes sense to keep a ready-made sauce on permanent standby. This recipe combines soy sauce, rice wine, sugar, sesame oil, garlic, and ginger—every flavor you want in a stir-fry dish. It pairs wonderfully with seafood and chicken, or as a sauce over noodles or rice.

SEASONING

½ cup Rich Homemade Broth (page 49) or canned chicken broth

¼ cup Chinese rice wine or dry sherry

1 tbsp. sesame oil

2 tsp. sugar

2 tsp. light soy sauce

½ tsp. salt

½ tsp. ground white pepper

2 tbsp. vegetable oil

1 tbsp. minced garlic

1 tbsp. minced ginger

1 tsp. cornstarch dissolved in 2 tsp. water

To make the seasoning, combine the broth, wine, sesame oil, sugar, soy sauce, salt, and white pepper in a small bowl and mix well.

Place a wok or stir-fry pan over high heat. Add the oil, swirling to coat the sides. Add the garlic and ginger and cook, stirring, until fragrant, about 20 seconds. Pour in the seasoning and cook, stirring, until the sugar dissolves. Add the cornstarch mixture and cook until the sauce boils and thickens, about 1 minute. Store in a covered container in the refrigerator; the sauce will keep for up to 1 week.

MAKES 1 CUP

All-Purpose Dark Stir-Fry Sauce

The oyster sauce gives this sauce a deeper flavor profile, which is perfect for dishes that call for a thicker, richer, more gravylike sauce. It works equally well with beef, chicken, vegetables, noodles, and rice—in other words, almost everything.

SEASONING

1 cup Rich Homemade Broth (page 49) or canned chicken broth

¼ cup oyster-flavored sauce

1 tbsp. dark soy sauce

1 tbsp. Chinese rice wine or dry sherry

1 tbsp. sesame oil

1 tsp. sugar

½ tsp. ground white pepper

2 tbsp. vegetable oil

1 tbsp. minced garlic

1 tbsp. minced ginger

1 tsp. cornstarch dissolved in 2 tsp. water

To make the seasoning, combine the broth, oyster sauce, soy sauce, wine, sesame oil, sugar, and white pepper in a small bowl and mix well.

Place a wok or stir-fry pan over high heat. Add the oil, swirling to coat the sides. Add the garlic and ginger and cook, stirring, until fragrant, about 20 seconds. Pour in the seasoning and cook, stirring, until the sugar dissolves. Add the cornstarch mixture and cook until the sauce boils and thickens, about 1 minute. Store in a covered container in the refrigerator; the sauce will keep for up to 1 week.

MAKES 1½ CUPS

Black Bean Sauce

Salted black beans might not be the most attractive ingredient in your kitchen, but they deliver a classic sauce. As this was one of my mother's favorite sauces, every time I smell black bean sauce, it brings me back to my old family kitchen in China.

SEASONING

½ cup Rich Homemade Broth (page 49) or canned chicken broth

2 tbsp. salted black beans, rinsed and lightly mashed

2 tbsp. Chinese rice wine or dry sherry

½ tsp. sugar

1 green onion, chopped

2 tbsp. vegetable oil

2 tbsp. finely shredded ginger

1 tbsp. minced garlic

1½ tsp. cornstarch dissolved in 1 tbsp. water

To make the seasoning, combine the broth, black beans, wine, sugar, and green onion in a small bowl and mix well.

Place a wok or stir-fry pan over high heat. Add the oil, swirling to coat the sides. Add the ginger and garlic and cook, stirring, until fragrant, about 20 seconds. Pour in the seasoning and cook, stirring, until the sugar dissolves. Add the cornstarch mixture and cook until the sauce boils and thickens, about 1 minute. Store in a covered container in the refrigerator; the sauce will keep for up to 1 week.

MAKES 1 CUP

General Tso Sauce

America might have its famous colonel, but when it comes to flavoring chicken, I still prefer my General Tso. Tso was a general from Hunan Province better known for his prowess with poultry than for his military maneuvers. Here's my philosophy: make dinner, not war!

SEASONING

¼ cup hoisin sauce

2 tbsp. regular soy sauce

1 tsp. dark soy sauce

2 tbsp. rice vinegar

2 tbsp. sugar

2 tsp. chili garlic sauce

1 tbsp. vegetable oil

1 tbsp. minced ginger

1 tsp. minced garlic

4 small dried red chiles, split lengthwise, or 1 tbsp. dried red chile flakes

1½ tsp. cornstarch dissolved in 1 tbsp. water

To make the seasoning, combine the hoisin sauce, regular and dark soy sauces, rice vinegar, sugar, and chili garlic sauce in a small bowl and mix well.

Place a wok or stir-fry pan over high heat. Add the oil, swirling to coat the sides. Add the ginger, garlic, and chiles and cook, stirring, until fragrant, about 20 seconds. Pour in the seasoning and cook, stirring, until the sugar dissolves. Add the cornstarch mixture and cook until the sauce boils and thickens, about 1 minute. Store in a covered container in the refrigerator; the sauce keeps for up to 1 week. Keep chiles in the sauce for more intense flavor.

MAKES 1 CUP

Mongolian Hoisin Sauce

Mongolia is a spectacular place, filled with natural wonders. Speaking of wonders, this rich and savory Mongolian sauce is a wonder all by itself. Try it on beef or lamb.

SEASONING

⅓ cup hoisin sauce

2 tbsp. Rich Homemade Broth (page 49) or canned chicken broth

4 tsp. chili bean sauce

1 tbsp. soy sauce

¼ tsp. sugar

1 tbsp. vegetable oil

2 tsp. minced garlic

2 tsp. minced ginger

To make the seasoning, combine the hoisin sauce, broth, chili bean sauce, soy sauce, and sugar in a small bowl and mix well.

Place a wok or stir-fry pan over high heat. Add the oil, swirling to coat the sides. Add the garlic and ginger and cook, stirring, until fragrant, about 20 seconds. Pour in the seasoning and cook, stirring, until the sugar dissolves. Store in a covered container in the refrigerator; it will keep for up to 2 weeks.

MAKES ¾ CUP

Another Face of China

Most Chinese feel a cultural kinship, and for good reason: ninety percent of us descend from Han Chinese. But the remaining ten percent equals 130 million people belonging to fifty-five ethnic groups, with distinctive heritage, languages, lifestyles, and cuisine. Fascinated visitors, like me, are drawn to Yunnan Province, the home of twenty-five of these.

At Lijiang County's Old Town, China's best-preserved ancient village, I found the Naxi tribe still practicing centuries-old customs. They call their shamans *dongba* (wise men) and also refer to religious texts, written in hieroglyphics, as *Dongba*. Rituals, as well as daily life, revolve around nature. The intricate network of canals carrying water from Jade Dragon Snow Mountain makes it easy to understand why they honor the mountain: its water is the lifeblood of this town.

At a local eatery, I sampled fries, sausage, and sticky rice with red bean powder, prepared the same way for centuries! Only the cook and customer were new.

Then a seventy-eight-year-old invited me on a mushroom hunt. I found myself panting to keep up with her. And she was one hot cook! She fearlessly stir-fried our harvest with a passel of chiles, pork, garlic chives, and green onions, serving it all with local chickpea noodles. I'm still savoring the memory of consuming that mushroom feast while enjoying a performance by Naxi's orchestra, world-famous for reviving Ming Dynasty music. My hosts, concerned that I might be growing hungry again, reassured me: "Don't worry; there's a banquet next!"

Early the next day, I traveled to Dali, home of the Bai people. As I dodged local "traffic" I realized that "horsepower" still means horses here. Colorfully dressed Bai elders were gathered in the town plaza keeping fit by practicing tai chi. The other secret to longevity everyone here under-

stands is, "Eat your vegetables!" I passed many family farms with scallions, carrots, potatoes, cabbage, green beans, eggplants, and chiles. Bai restaurants like to display fresh produce outside, including wild ingredients like golden lily and wood ear mushrooms.

My Bai hosts welcomed me with traditional dances and an orchestra performance by budding and talented senior musicians. They prepared a plum banquet to honor my visit. And all the dishes were plumb good! We toasted with home-brewed plum wine. The qualities of salted plum—salty, bitter, and sweet—symbolize the Bai philosophy: contrasts make for a stimulating life. Maybe that accounts for their kind, patient spirit.

I'd heard stories about remote Lugu Lake's "kingdom of women," and it's true: Musuo women rule the roost! Female elders govern. Women head households and prefer not to marry. Children are raised by their mothers, with maternal uncles providing male support. Mount Shizi is considered their goddess, and the surrounding "male" mountains her lovers. I tried to cozy up to her, but she was stone cold.

Inside a Musuo home, the head of the household sits beside the fire, while others sit farther away. As a man, I was honored to be in this room. But not for long! Ordered to pitch in on a construction project, I rolled up my sleeves. Like all village men, I had to earn my lunch. It was worth it: a home-cooked meal with garden vegetables and fish just caught in Lugu Lake. Of course, the Musuo call her Mother Lake!

All of my new indigenous friends inspired me with their wonderful sense of community. They're keepers of the flame—and I don't mean in the fireplace. They keep sacred traditions alive, from generation to generation, century after century.

Orange Sauce

I always find the taste of citrus enticing; it can add much freshness to a dish. This sauce is a perfect alternative to sweet-and-sour sauce. Try it in your stir-fried chicken or pork dish and you'll have elegance on a plate, ready to impress your dinner guests every time.

SEASONING

¼ cup freshly squeezed orange juice

2 tbsp. minced fresh orange zest

2 green onions, chopped

3 tbsp. Rich Homemade Broth (page 49) or canned chicken broth

1 tbsp. soy sauce

2 tsp. Chinese rice wine or dry sherry

2 tsp. sesame oil

1 tsp. rice vinegar

5 tsp. sugar

⅛ tsp. ground white pepper

1 tbsp. vegetable oil

4 small dried red chiles, or 1 tbsp. red chile flakes

2 tsp. minced garlic

2 tsp. minced ginger

1 tsp. cornstarch dissolved in 2 tsp. water

To make the seasoning, combine the orange juice and zest, green onions, broth, soy sauce, wine, sesame oil, rice vinegar, sugar, and white pepper in a small bowl and mix well.

Place a wok or stir-fry pan over high heat. Add the oil, swirling to coat the sides. Add the chiles, garlic, and ginger and cook, stirring, until fragrant, about 20 seconds. Pour in the seasoning and cook, stirring, until the sugar dissolves. Add the cornstarch mixture and cook until the sauce boils and thickens, about 1 minute. Store in a covered container in the refrigerator; the sauce will keep for up to 1 week. Discard chiles after cooking or keep in the sauce for spicier flavor.

MAKES ¾ CUP

Sichuan Kung Pao Sauce

A viewer once wrote, "Martin, can you kung pao everything?" Well, maybe not everything, but close. *Kung pao* is probably the best known of all Sichuan-Hunan sauces. Its combination of hot, sour, sweet, and savory is the very embodiment of sophistication and substance.

SEASONING

¼ cup Chinese black vinegar or balsamic vinegar

¼ cup Rich Homemade Broth (page 49) or canned chicken broth

3 tbsp. Chinese rice wine or dry sherry

2 tbsp. sugar

1 tbsp. sesame oil

2 tsp. soy sauce

2 tsp. chili garlic sauce

1 tbsp. vegetable oil

8 small dried red chiles

1 tsp. cornstarch dissolved in 2 tsp. water

To make the seasoning, combine the vinegar, broth, wine, sugar, sesame oil, soy sauce, and chili garlic sauce in a small bowl and mix well.

Place a wok or stir-fry pan over high heat. Add the oil, swirling to coat the sides. Add the chiles and cook, stirring, until fragrant, about 20 seconds. Pour in the seasoning and cook, stirring, until the sugar dissolves. Add the cornstarch mixture and cook until the sauce boils and thickens, about 1 minute. Store in a covered container in the refrigerator; it will keep for up to 2 weeks.

MAKES 1 CUP

Sweet-and-Sour Sauce

....

When asked to name one dish on the Chinese menu that has conquered the West, most people will say sweet-and-sour! For generations, this simple flavor combination embodied Chinese food for most of the world. In China, sweet-and-sour is typically used as a dipping sauce and is made with sugar or honey and rice vinegar. I've added orange juice to this recipe to lighten up the sauce, and also a little chile oil to give it a kick.

SEASONING	5 tbsp. ketchup	1 tbsp. vegetable oil
¼ cup fresh orange juice	2 tsp. soy sauce	1 tsp. minced ginger
¼ cup rice vinegar	1 tbsp. minced hot green chile, such as jalapeño or serrano	1½ tbsp. cornstarch dissolved in 3 tbsp. water
5 tbsp. packed brown sugar		

....

To make the seasoning, combine the orange juice, vinegar, brown sugar, ketchup, soy sauce, and chile in a bowl and mix well.

Place a wok or stir-fry pan over high heat. Add the oil, swirling to coat the sides. Add the ginger and cook, stirring, until fragrant, about 20 seconds. Pour in the seasoning and cook, stirring, until the sugar dissolves. Add the cornstarch mixture and cook until the sauce boils and thickens, about 1 minute. Store in a covered container in the refrigerator; it will keep for up to 1 week.

MAKES ABOUT 1½ CUPS

Rich Homemade Broth

A good broth has saved the reputation of countless chefs and home cooks. In a professional kitchen, two different types of stock are made: a more flavor-intense version for sauces and a delicate one for soups. This recipe is the best of both versions. The savory flavor of this broth is enhanced by the unique addition of Smithfield ham.

One 3- to 4-pound whole chicken	3 pounds lean pork, such as loin
8 ounces Smithfield ham	8 cups cold water

Rinse the chicken, inside and out, under cold water. Rinse the Smithfield ham under cold water to remove excess salt.

Place the chicken, ham, and pork in a large pot. Add enough water to cover by 1 inch. Bring to a boil over high heat and let boil for 5 minutes. Drain, discarding the liquid. Rinse the chicken, ham, and pork and drain, discarding the liquid.

Return the meats to a clean pot and add the 8 cups water. Bring just to a boil over high heat. Reduce the heat to maintain a gentle simmer. Skim any foam that rises to the surface. Cook covered until the chicken is falling off the bone, about 2 hours.

Strain through a fine-mesh sieve, saving the meat for another use.

Use immediately or let cool, cover, and refrigerate for up to 1 week or freeze for up to 6 months.

MAKES 8 CUPS

STOCK TIPS

"I am lucky to have dined in the world's finest Chinese restaurants. What sets their amazing dishes apart from less stellar creations is not their final assembly, but their foundation . . . the soup stock. It's the basis of exceptional savory dishes from Paris to Beijing. Great Chinese stock starts with chicken, lean pork, pork bones, selected cured meat, ginger, and green onion. After simmering for several hours, the liquid covering these ingredients reduces to a rich stock infused with intense flavors. Pre-prepared stock can be readily used in soups, stir-fries, and many other dishes."

On the Road

Early in life, I learned an old Chinese proverb: "The knowledge in ten thousand books cannot equal a journey of ten thousand miles." Over the years, that saying has proven true, time and time again. I read plenty of books about China, but it wasn't until I began traveling to its many regions that I gained true insight into the land and its people. On these trips, I've met many remarkable characters, all with unique life experiences and customs. They showed me things I could never have learned with my nose in a book.

From Guangdong to Sichuan, Beijing, Shanghai, Lijiang, Guilin, Shanxi, and Shangri-la to the towns in the foothills of the Himalayas, I've gotten to know China as a diverse collection of cultures and communities. Maybe you think traveling through China is easy for me, a native son. To be honest, I'd be lost without a guide and a good interpreter. In the United States, I can drive from Los Angeles to New York without a bit of culture shock. In China, I drive a few hours and it's like entering a completely new world, with distinct customs, architecture, landscape, and food.

Did I mention the language barrier? In the city of Guangzhou alone, there are more than two dozen distinct dialects. Within a hundred kilometers, that number jumps to dozens more. Granted, everybody is supposed to speak Mandarin these days, but speak it with an accent that, shall we say, only their mothers could love.

People's food and dietary habits never cease to astonish me. I discovered, for instance, that Shanxi people make noodles in a very theatri-cal way. It's like a beautiful performance piece. That area seems to be wine/vinegar/noodle central! Local inhabitants developed the art of winemaking more than four thousand years ago and have been perfecting vinegar production for nearly three thousand years. Their aged vinegar is almost a match for balsamic. In Shangri-la, I was urged to join in a daily ritual of swallowing a spoonful of wild, toasted wheat while sipping yak butter tea. I was warned not to breathe until the mixture went down, a tip I learned to appreciate too late, after a good, long choke.

Cultural and linguistic differences may be obstacles at times, but they are also what makes exploring China so exciting. In the ancient town of Lijiang, I witnessed age-old tribal ways of life, still in practice. At picturesque Lugu Lake, I found myself getting bossed around by women in the last matriarchal village. I have seen exotic outfits, exquisite arts, and unusual rituals beyond my wildest imaginings. As I explored these fasci-nating cultures-within-a-culture, I developed an appreciation for local customs and became more conscious of how I carried myself. As a guest, it's important to know where to sit and how to inter-act socially. I've ridden horseback with Malay-sian cowboys and danced with nimble grandmas, mastered the art of steamed wheat buns under the guidance of a northern farmer's wife, joined Hong Kong fishermen on an expedition, and helped a tribal chief roast wild mountain pig on a spit. Every day of travel brings new friends, new ad-ventures . . . and culinary surprises!

Soy-Vinegar Dipping Sauce

....

Add more jalapeño to bring up the spice, or you can omit it altogether. This multipurpose dipping sauce can be used for the Green Onion and Garlic Pancakes (page 74), used as a sauce for simply poached fish, or spooned over steamed rice. Add a few drops of sesame oil for another flavor dimension.

½ cup soy sauce

¼ cup rice vinegar

2 green onions, finely chopped

1 tbsp. minced hot green chile, such as jalapeño or serrano

1 tbsp. minced garlic

....

In a small bowl, combine all the ingredients and stir until mixed. Store in a covered container in the refrigerator; it will keep for up to 1 week.

MAKES ¾ CUP

Mustard Dipping Sauce

....

I was asked if there's a difference between American mustard and its Chinese cousin. One taste and you can tell that they are cousins many times removed. The Chinese version is a lot more pungent. It is available in powdered or paste form. If Chinese mustard is not available, use the Dijon variety.

3 tbsp. mustard powder

3 tbsp. honey

2 tbsp. fresh lemon juice

2 tbsp. rice vinegar

2 tbsp. soy sauce

....

Combine all the ingredients in a small bowl and whisk until the honey dissolves. Store in a covered container in the refrigerator; it will keep for up to 1 week.

MAKES ¾ CUP

Beijing Dipping Sauce

This one is as bold as it is versatile: you can mix it into salad dressings, toss it with noodles for a fiery and tasty side dish, and use it on grilled meats, such as my New Beijing Lamb (page 190).

½ cup sweet chili sauce

2 tbsp. fish sauce

2 tsp. chili garlic sauce

2 tbsp. chopped fresh mint

2 tsp. minced garlic

1 tsp. soy sauce

2 tsp. water

In a bowl, combine all the ingredients and stir until well mixed. Store in a covered container in the refrigerator; it will keep for up to 1 week.

MAKES ¾ CUP

Sweet Plum Vinaigrette

....

Chinese cooks can think of 101 uses for plum sauce and are taking advantage of the unique tart and sweet flavor to brighten up salads. This spicy and tangy vinaigrette works wonders on greens or for grilled meats.

⅔ cup vegetable oil	1 tbsp. hoisin sauce	1 tsp. minced ginger
⅓ cup rice vinegar	1 tbsp. honey	1 tsp. salt
2 tbsp. plum sauce	2 green onions, minced	¼ tsp. Chinese five-spice powder

....

In a small bowl, combine all the ingredients and whisk until blended. Store in a covered container in the refrigerator; it will keep for up to 1 week. Bring to room temperature and stir before using.

MAKES ABOUT 1¼ CUPS

Asian Vinaigrette

....

The Chinese love vegetables but usually prefer them cooked instead of raw. However, after decades of living in North America, I have adapted my diet to include salad. In fact, our family eats a lot of salads, all thanks to this dressing.

⅔ cup vegetable oil	1 tsp. Chili Oil (page 58) or store-bought chili oil	1 small shallot, finely chopped
5 tbsp. rice vinegar	2 tsp. minced garlic	1 tbsp. chopped cilantro
2 tbsp. ketchup	1 tsp. minced ginger	½ tsp. mustard powder
1 tbsp. soy sauce	1 green onion, finely chopped	⅛ tsp. ground white pepper
1 tbsp. honey		
1 tsp. sesame oil		

....

In a medium bowl, combine all the ingredients and whisk until the honey dissolves. Store in a covered container in the refrigerator; the vinaigrette will keep for up to 3 weeks. Bring to room temperature and stir before using.

MAKES ABOUT 1¼ CUPS

Chef Yan's Chili Sauce

Every cook needs a good, all-purpose chili sauce, and this is mine. I like strong flavors, so I load it up with lots of garlic, chiles, and dried shrimp. Yum! Use this sauce as a condiment or in cooking to enhance the flavor of fish, meats, vegetables, and blander foods such as tofu or noodles. Add a bit of this to fried rice and it'll perk up the flavor.

1 cup dried red chiles, stems removed

1½ cups boiling water

¼ cup small dried shrimp

⅓ cup peanut oil

¼ cup minced garlic

¼ cup minced shallots

1 tbsp. finely diced Smithfield ham

1 tsp. sugar

Rinse the chiles and drain. Place in a medium bowl and add 1 cup of the boiling water. Let sit until the chiles are rehydrated, about 30 minutes. Meanwhile, place the shrimp in a small bowl and add the remaining ½ cup boiling water. Let sit until the shrimp are rehydrated, about 30 minutes. Drain the shrimp well and transfer to a plate lined with paper towels to soak up the excess moisture.

Transfer the shrimp and the chiles with their soaking water to a food processor or blender and process until puréed. Set aside.

Place a wok or stir-fry pan over medium-high heat. Add the oil, swirling to coat the sides. Add the garlic and shallots and cook, stirring, until they are lightly golden, about 2 minutes. Add the ham, the puréed shrimp and chiles, and sugar, standing back to avoid the splatter. Continue to cook, stirring constantly, until the water evaporates and the sauce thickens, 6 to 7 minutes.

Transfer the sauce to a small, heatproof bowl and set aside to let cool. Store in a covered container in the refrigerator; it will keep for up to 2 weeks. Bring to room temperature and stir before using.

MAKES 1¼ CUPS

Peanut Dressing

You don't have to be choosy to choose homemade peanut dressing. It's simple to make and you can create different flavors by substituting other nut butters, such as almond or cashew. Make it a family project with the kids. You may want to add a bit of sugar or honey to round out the flavor. This dressing also works well as a dipping sauce, or for basting grilled chicken during the last minutes of cooking.

2 tsp. vegetable oil

1 clove garlic, minced

⅔ cup Rich Homemade Broth (page 49) or canned chicken broth

¼ cup hoisin sauce

3 tbsp. smooth peanut butter

1 tbsp. fish sauce

1 tsp. chili garlic sauce

¼ cup unsalted roasted peanuts, chopped

Place a small saucepan over medium-high heat until hot. Add the oil, swirling to coat the bottom. Add the garlic and cook, stirring, until fragrant, about 10 seconds. Add the broth, hoisin sauce, peanut butter, fish sauce, and chili garlic sauce and bring to a boil. Reduce the heat to low, and simmer until thickened, 4 to 5 minutes. Stir in the peanuts. Serve the dressing hot, warm, or at room temperature. Store in a covered container in the refrigerator; it will keep for up to 2 weeks.

MAKES 1¼ CUPS

Chili Oil

Do not confuse this with vegetable oil, which is commonly used for stir-frying and deep-frying food. Chili oil is a flavoring agent; a little of this will go a long way. Add it to dressings and sauces to give them a spicy finish, or use it as a dipping sauce for dumplings. Like sesame oil, chili oil is widely available in stores, but I prefer to make my own. It's really quite easy, and you can control the level of hotness.

2 cups vegetable oil

1 cup dried red chile flakes

In a 1-quart pan, combine the oil and chile flakes. Heat over medium-low heat until the chiles have infused the oil with their flavor, about 20 minutes. Remove the pan from the heat and set aside to cool completely. Let sit at room temperature overnight for a stronger chile flavor.

Strain the chili oil through a fine sieve into a glass jar. The oil will keep at room temperature for up to 1 month.

MAKES 2 CUPS

Cilantro Oil

Here's something that truly separates the great home cooks from the great home cooks who are deprived of the joy of cilantro oil. If you love cilantro as much as I do, try making your own cilantro oil. By the way, I use this same technique to make basil, parsley, and chive oils. There's never an oil embargo in my kitchen.

1 bunch fresh cilantro, cleaned and thoroughly dried

¾ cup vegetable oil

Coarsely chop the cilantro and add it to the bowl of a blender. Add the oil and blend on high speed until puréed. Transfer the purée to a nonreactive bowl, cover, and refrigerate overnight.

The following day, strain the purée through a double layer of cheesecloth, squeezing out as much oil as possible, into a clean bowl. Store in a covered container in the refrigerator; it will keep for up to 1 week.

MAKES ABOUT ¾ CUP

CHILI OIL

CILANTRO OIL

Steamed White Rice

As a native of Southern China, I am a "rice-aholic." To me, no Chinese meal is complete without rice. I often cook a large batch so I will have leftovers. Why? The secret to great fried rice is cold rice. Freshly cooked rice will stick to the bottom of the wok when you fry it. Making the perfect steamed rice is easy: follow my recipe or, if you have a rice cooker, follow the manufacturer's instructions.

2 cups long-grain white rice   3 cups water

Place the rice in a sieve and rinse under cold running water until the water runs clear. Drain well.

Place the rice in a 3-quart saucepan with a tight-fitting lid. Add the water and bring to a boil over high heat. Cook, uncovered, until craterlike holes form on the surface of the rice and most of the water has evaporated, 6 to 8 minutes. Reduce the heat to low, cover, and cook, undisturbed, for 10 minutes.

Remove from the heat and let the rice stand, covered, for a few minutes. Remove the cover, fluff the rice with a fork, and serve.

MAKES ABOUT 5½ CUPS

Steamed Brown Rice

Brown rice is unmilled or partly milled rice. It has a mild, nutty flavor and a chewier texture than white rice. Nutritionists advocate brown rice for its health benefits. There are many types of brown rice today, such as brown jasmine, long-grain brown, and short-grain brown.

1 ½ cups brown rice,   2 ½ cups water
long-grain or jasmine

Place the rice in a sieve and rinse under cold running water until the water runs clear. Drain well.

Place the rice in a 3-quart saucepan with a tight-fitting lid. Add the water and bring to a boil over high heat. Cook, uncovered, until craterlike holes form on the surface of the rice and most of the water has evaporated, 6 to 8 minutes. Reduce the heat to low, cover, and cook, undisturbed, for 10 minutes.

Remove from the heat and let the rice stand, covered, for a few minutes. Remove the cover, fluff the rice with a fork, and serve.

MAKES ABOUT 4 CUPS

SIK FAN MEI AH?

In Mandarin, it's *"Chi le fan mei you?"*
In Cantonese, it's *"Sik fan mei ah?"*
Both mean "Have you eaten yet?" Over centuries, this
has become a common expression,
equivalent to "How are you?"

This traditional greeting shows not only the cultural
significance of food but also the Chinese belief that
how you are has to do with whether you've eaten.

It's an appropriate social exchange because
eating is a social event. In China, connections
and friendships are forged over food.

Spicy Pickled Cucumbers

This is a real appetite pick-me-up in salads, as a side dish, or as an appetizer (the Chinese version of antipasto). You can peel the cucumbers completely (which will make them a bit softer), peel them partially (in stripes), or pickle them without peeling. What can I say? Do what "appeals" to you.

1 English cucumber	2 tbsp. soy sauce	1 or 2 small fresh red chiles, stemmed and thinly sliced
1 tsp. salt	2 tbsp. sugar	
½ cup rice vinegar		

Cut the cucumber in half lengthwise and then thinly slice each half on the diagonal.

In a bowl, combine the cucumber and salt, toss to mix, and let stand for 10 minutes. Rinse, drain, pat dry, and place in a medium bowl. Combine the vinegar, soy sauce, sugar, and chiles in a small glass bowl, stirring until the sugar dissolves. Add the vinegar mixture to the cucumbers. Cover and set aside for 1 hour. Store in a covered container in the refrigerator; the cucumbers will keep for up to 1 week.

MAKES 4 CUPS

Roasted Garlic

When you roast garlic, it becomes sweet and caramelized. Roasted garlic can be left whole and tossed into salads and sauces or mashed and stirred into dressings. Roast a few heads at a time. Your kitchen will smell like an Italian restaurant.

1 head garlic	Pinch of salt
1 tbsp. vegetable oil	Pinch of ground black pepper

Preheat the oven to 400 degrees F.

Cut the stem end (the pointed end) off of the garlic head, about ¼ of the way down. Put the garlic head, root side (flat side) down, in the center of an 8-inch square of aluminum foil. Drizzle the oil over the cut side of the garlic. Season with salt and pepper. Gather the corners of the foil together to completely enclose the garlic head. Roast until the garlic cloves are golden brown and caramelized, 35 to 45 minutes.

Remove the garlic head from the oven. When cool enough to handle, about 10 minutes, carefully remove the foil and squeeze the garlic head, cut side facing down, to remove the cloves. Discard the garlic skins.

MAKES 1 HEAD

Pickled Vegetables

With this recipe, you will have no problem convincing your kids or anyone else to load up on veggies. The fresh red and green jalapeño chiles make this dish anything but bland.

2 red bell peppers

½ cabbage

½ jicama, or 8 ounces canned whole water chestnuts, cut in half

1 green jalapeño chile

1 red jalapeño chile

6-inch piece daikon, thinly sliced

1 carrot, sliced

10 slices ginger

8 walnut-sized shallots, thinly sliced

2 tsp. salt

PICKLING SOLUTION

1 tbsp. Sichuan peppercorns, toasted

2 cups rice vinegar

1¼ cups sugar

1¼ tsp. salt

½ tsp. dried red chile flakes

Cut the bell peppers, cabbage, and jicama into 1- to 1½-inch chunks. Cut the green and red jalapeños in half and discard the seeds.

Place the bell peppers, cabbage, jicama, jalapeños, daikon, carrot, ginger, and shallots in a large bowl; rub the salt into them with your hands. Cover the vegetables with a plate, weight it with a heavy can, and let stand at room temperature for 1 hour.

Place all of the ingredients for the pickling solution into a saucepan. Cook, stirring, over medium-high heat until the sugar dissolves, 2 to 3 minutes. Let stand until cool.

Pour the vegetable mixture into a colander and rinse well to remove the salty liquid. Place the vegetables in a self-sealing plastic bag or in a nonreactive bowl. Pour the cooled pickling solution over the vegetables. Seal the bag or cover the bowl with plastic wrap. Refrigerate for at least 2 days or up to a week.

MAKES 6 CUPS

A PICKLE OF A SITUATION—AND LOVING IT!

Driving through China with my film crew, we could smell when a pickle factory was close. It gave me mouthwatering thoughts of Chinese pickles in stir-fries, soups, and table condiments. In the West, a pickle is usually a preserved cucumber, but in China, it can be any fruit or vegetable.

Before refrigeration, foods piled up during harvest. It was a pickle of a situation! So the early Chinese developed preservation techniques, including drying, curing, fermenting, and pickling—methods still in use today. Pickling uses salt, vinegar, and sugar as preservatives.

Shrimp Mousse

Traditional recipes for shrimp mousse require pork fat to add moisture and tenderness to the mixture. For a lighter approach, I recommend using soft tofu. You can also add fish to the shrimp mixture, or make it an all-fish mousse if you fancy. I recommend a mild white-fleshed fish, such as halibut or cod. Seafood pastes are commonly stuffed into peppers, formed into balls to poach or deep-fry for soups and stir-fries, and even used as fillings for dumplings. They're delicious whichever way you want to cook them.

3 green onions, white parts only, coarsely chopped

2 cloves garlic, peeled and coarsely chopped

2 tsp. chopped ginger

10 ounces medium-sized raw shrimp, peeled and deveined

1 egg white

2 tbsp. soft tofu

1 tbsp. soy sauce

1 tsp. sesame oil

1 tsp. cornstarch

¼ tsp. salt

⅛ tsp. ground white pepper

Put the green onions, garlic, and ginger in the bowl of a food processor and pulse until minced. Add the shrimp, egg white, tofu, soy sauce, sesame oil, cornstarch, salt, and white pepper. Pulse 5 times to finely chop all of the ingredients, then pulse in 5-second intervals until a very smooth paste forms. The mousse can be stored in a covered container in the refrigerator for up to 2 days.

MAKES ABOUT 1 CUP

Preserved Duck Legs

Before the invention of refrigeration, every cuisine had its unique way of preserving meat. The French are famous for their confit, which is meat that has been cooked slowly in its own fat.

This recipe is "confit-inspired," but the spices and aromas are purely Chinese. Add this duck to any noodle, rice, or stir-fried vegetable dish and let its succulent flavor and silky texture work magic.

SEASONING

1 tsp. Chinese five-spice powder

1 tsp. ground ginger

1 tsp. ground nutmeg

1 tsp. ground white pepper

1 tbsp. salt

4 whole duck legs

5 cups duck fat or vegetable oil

To make the seasoning, combine the five-spice powder, ginger, nutmeg, white pepper, and salt in a small bowl.

Generously coat each duck leg with some of the seasoning. Place the legs, skin side up, on a rack set over a baking sheet. Cover loosely with plastic wrap and refrigerate for 2 days.

Transfer the duck legs to a 2-quart saucepan. Add enough duck fat to completely submerge the legs. Heat over low heat and simmer very gently until the legs are thoroughly cooked through, about 2 hours.

Store in a covered container, being sure the legs are completely submerged in the fat; it will keep for up to 2 months.

MAKES 4 DUCK LEGS

East and West Culinary Arts Exchange

Until the past century, to most people, a trip of a couple hundred miles was the journey of a lifetime. With no phones, cars, airplanes, or computers, little exchange took place, even between neighboring provinces. This isolation gave rise to distinct customs and cuisines, often within the same country.

China's civilization dates back thousands of years, and over time, four classic regional cuisines developed: Mandarin in the north, Shanghai in the east, Cantonese in the south, and Sichuan in the west. When natives of one region migrated to another, they brought their favorite recipes and cooking techniques with them. But because of different climates and the availability of different ingredients, traditional dishes from one region often underwent a transformation in their new home. Although purists might disapprove, I think these deviations were healthy and contributed to the long-term survival of each cuisine.

China took pride in being the "Middle Kingdom," in much the same way that ancient Rome considered itself the center of the civilized world. Outsiders—and in the case of China that included millions of minority peoples living within its borders—could only benefit from assimilating the culture of the Middle Kingdom, including all its rich culinary traditions. The truth is, chefs within the Middle Kingdom had long been benefiting from contact with the outside world. As far back as the second century B.C., Chinese chefs were experimenting with ingredients from Central Asia and Eastern Europe, while the outside world was simultaneously developing a craving for Asian flavors. How? Two words: Silk Road, the first route to link Imperial China to the Roman Empire.

Now fast-forward two thousand years. As Chinese immigrants began to settle abroad in earnest, many transplanted Chinese chefs adapted their recipes to foreign tastes, creating imaginative Chinese dishes that incorporated Western ingredients, techniques, and seasonings. At the same time, Western chefs began to appreciate Chinese ingredients, techniques, and seasonings. In the past decade, these culinary exchanges have escalated at a furious pace, leading to a new cooking style with a trendy label: *fusion*!

Today, you see a subtle shift occurring in the culinary arts of every culture. Someone in Southern China can order an English breakfast, have a French bistro lunch, and later settle down for a dinner of Peking duck. I think it's great that everybody's palate is being expanded and refined. It's common now to find seasonings and exotic ingredients from faraway countries in the pantries of home kitchens. This is the result of the ever-increasing culinary exchange between chefs internationally. As they share the best of their traditions, including recipes, techniques, and skills, we all reap the benefits.

For the past fifteen years, I have been fortunate to be a part of this evolution, introducing classic Chinese cuisine to professional chefs and food enthusiasts from around the world. Every year, my Yan Can Cook team and I organize gourmet tours to many different parts of China and Asia. To fulfill the increasing number of requests for short-term, intensive courses and food lectures, Chef Martin Yan's Culinary Arts Center in Shenzhen, China, opened its doors in 2007. Now professional chefs and leisure cooks alike can visit the center to learn and discover the fine art of Chinese cuisine, developed over the course of five thousand years. At the same time, visitors can explore this ancient civilization's fascinating historical sites and enjoy its cultural highlights.

Appetizers
& Soups

With increased traveling opportunities and cultural exchanges, chefs in China are becoming more educated in international cuisine. This has spurred a new wave of Chinese cooking, incorporating new cooking techniques, ingredients, and ways of presentation.

Many modern Chinese restaurants are beginning to serve appetizers as a separate course to start the meal. In the past, they were served as side dishes, along with entrées, to add texture and flavor to the meal. The exception to this is a formal banquet setting, in which each course is brought to the table separately.

In a way, the concept of appetizers is not really revolutionary in China. In every city and town, one of the most common (and, for me, welcoming) sights is street food. From a simple lamb skewer on the grill to a bowl of delicious *dan dan* noodles, you can enjoy a wide variety of food anytime, day or night. Many Chinese eat them as a snack, a quick pick-me-up before heading home for dinner. In other words, as appetizers!

In this chapter I have included, some old standbys like Green Onion and Garlic Pancakes (page 74) and Crispy Spring Rolls (page 75). For those who like a little culinary excitement, I added Street-Style Crispy Chicken (page 72). I discovered that dish in the streets of Guangzhou and found it truly addictive. Speaking of chicken, on Nanjing Road in Shanghai, a "chicken war" is being waged. Inspired by the success of a newly arrived chicken franchise, street vendors are offering local variations. The last time I visited Nanjing Road, both chicken camps were doing a brisk business. I guess in Shanghai, there's never a need for chicken lovers to cross the road.

In many parts of China, dairy products are not all that popular. Such is not the case in the north and west of the country, however. Many minority communities in western Yunnan and Sichuan Provinces commonly consume yak milk and cheese in their diet. When I saw a local version of a cheese sandwich, I was inspired to reinvent my own version, naming it the Martin Cristo (page 84).

Great as starters before a meal or as a meal in themselves, these appetizers fit perfectly into our multi-dimensional lifestyles.

Poached Eggplant with Spicy Peanut Sauce

How's this for a misnomer? An eggplant contains no egg, and in fact, it's a fruit! Technically, it's a big berry, but I won't be looking for eggplant ice cream or yogurt anytime soon. The Chinese like to oil-blanch, steam, or boil eggplants. Some people don't care for the skin, but I like it for texture and flavor.

3 quarter-sized slices ginger, lightly crushed	Leaves from 1 bunch cilantro	⅓ cup Peanut Dressing (page 57)
3 green onions, chopped	Cloves from 1 head Roasted Garlic (page 62), skins removed	2 tbsp. Cilantro Oil (page 58)
1 tbsp. salt		
3 Asian eggplants		

Fill a large, deep pot with water and bring to a boil over high heat. Add the ginger, green onions, and salt, and boil for 1 minute. Add the eggplants and cook, turning occasionally, until they are just cooked through and tender when pierced with the tip of a sharp knife, 6 to 10 minutes, depending on the thickness of the eggplant. Drain, discarding the green onions and ginger.

Trim the stems from the eggplants, and peel off the skin, using your fingers or a paring knife. Discard the skin. Transfer the eggplants to a plate or wide, shallow bowl. Using 2 forks, shred the eggplant meat into long, thin strips. Or you can cut the eggplant into ¼-inch-thick rounds. Toss with the cilantro leaves, roasted garlic, and half of the peanut dressing.

Transfer to a serving plate. Spoon the remaining dressing over the eggplant, and drizzle the cilantro oil over all.

MAKES 4 TO 6 SERVINGS

Street-Style Crispy Chicken

While visiting Guangzhou, I came across a street vendor selling crispy little nuggets of chicken flavored with red fermented bean curd. How unusual! And how absolutely delicious! Typically, bean curd is fermented in rice wine and chiles. I like the intense flavor of red fermented bean curd for cooking or marinating.

MARINADE

2 cubes (about 1 ounce) red fermented bean curd

¼ tsp. sugar

¼ tsp. salt

⅛ tsp. ground white pepper

1 pound boneless chicken thighs, cut into ½-inch-wide strips

Vegetable oil for deep-frying

2 tbsp. cornstarch

1 egg

1 green onion, green part only, chopped

To make the marinade, in a medium bowl mash the bean curd to a paste with the tines of a fork. Add the sugar, salt, and white pepper and mix well. Add the chicken, cover, and marinate in the refrigerator for 1 hour or up to 4 hours.

Pour the oil into a wok, stir-fry pan, or 2-quart saucepan to a depth of 2 inches and heat to 350 degrees F. Mix the cornstarch and egg with a whisk in a medium bowl. Add the chicken and stir to coat evenly. Working in batches, deep-fry the chicken, stirring gently to prevent the pieces from sticking together, until golden brown and crisp, about 5 minutes per batch. Remove with a wire strainer or slotted spoon and place on paper towels to drain.

Divide the chicken among 4 parchment paper cones, little brown paper bags, or individual bowls. Garnish each with some of the green onion and serve.

MAKES 4 SERVINGS

Green Onion and Garlic Pancakes

You won't find this on the menu of your neighborhood pancake house. Go to Northern China, however, and you'll see green onion pancakes everywhere you look. Just bite into these unleavened fried breads and you'll see why. They are crispy on the outside, moist and chewy inside, and bursting with onion and roasted garlic flavor. If you're a true garlic fan, roast your own. Otherwise, use 2 tbsp. of minced garlic, either raw or sautéed in a little oil.

DOUGH

2¼ cups all-purpose flour

¾ cup cold water, plus more as needed

FILLING

½ cup plus 2 tbsp. lard or vegetable shortening

Cloves from 1 head Roasted Garlic (page 62), skins removed

3 green onions, green parts only, thinly sliced

2 tsp. sesame oil

1½ tsp. salt

½ cup plus 1 tbsp. vegetable oil

To make the dough, sift the flour into a large mixing bowl. Add ¾ cup cold water and stir with a wooden spoon until a soft dough forms. Add a few more tsp. of water to the dough if it seems too stiff. Turn the dough out onto a lightly floured surface and knead until it is smooth, about 5 minutes. Cover with plastic wrap and set aside to rest for 15 minutes.

To make the filling, mash the lard and roasted garlic together in a medium bowl with the back of a wooden spoon until a smooth paste forms. Add the green onions, sesame oil, and salt and stir until well mixed.

Unwrap the dough and cut it into 15 equal portions. Roll each piece of dough into a 1-inch-thick cylinder. Using a pastry brush, lightly oil a smooth surface with some of the vegetable oil. Roll a cylinder out to a 3-by-10-inch strip of dough. Spread 1 heaping tbsp. of the filling across the entire surface of the dough. Starting from one end, fold the strip of dough diagonally, as you would fold a flag, up and over the filling, until you have a compact triangle of dough. Pinch the seam shut and shape into a 1½-inch round disk. Repeat with the remaining dough and filling.

Heat a large, nonstick skillet over medium heat. Add the ½ cup of vegetable oil and heat until hot. Put about half of the cakes into the hot oil; they should not touch. Cover and fry until golden brown and crisp, about 5 minutes. Flip the cakes and continue to cook, uncovered, until golden brown on the second side. Repeat the process with the remaining cakes, adding more oil if necessary.

Transfer to a serving plate and serve.

MAKES 15 CAKES

Crispy Spring Rolls

Not to be confused with egg rolls, their husky, Chinese American cousins, spring rolls are slimmer in size and crispier on their exterior. They're popular in China during the Spring Festival, but personally, I think they are the perfect finger food for all seasons.

FILLING

8 ounces ground pork or chicken

2 tbsp. minced green onion

1 tbsp. minced water chestnut

1 tbsp. minced cilantro

½ tsp. minced garlic

1 tsp. sesame oil

1 tsp. fish sauce

½ tsp. soy sauce

1 tsp. salt

½ tsp. sugar

⅛ tsp. ground white pepper

Six 6-inch square spring roll wrappers, cut into fourths

1 egg, lightly beaten with 1 tbsp. water

Vegetable oil for deep-frying

½ cup Sweet-and-Sour Sauce (page 48) or a store-bought version

To make the filling, in a large bowl, combine the ground pork, green onion, water chestnut, cilantro, garlic, sesame oil, fish sauce, soy sauce, salt, sugar, and white pepper, and mix well.

To make each roll, place a wrapper on a work surface with one of the corners facing you. Spread a tbsp. of the filling on the bottom third of the wrapper. Fold the bottom edge of the wrapper over the filling, then fold in the right and left corners. Roll over once to enclose the filling. Brush the sides with some of the egg mixture. Fold over to seal. Cover with a damp kitchen towel to prevent them from drying out.

Pour oil to a depth of 2 inches into a wok or stir-fry pan. Heat over high heat to 350 degrees F on a deep-fry thermometer. Working in batches, add the rolls and deep-fry, turning the rolls until they are golden brown and the filling is cooked, about 2 minutes. Remove with a wire strainer or a slotted spoon and drain on paper towels.

Serve the rolls warm with the sauce on the side.

MAKES 24 ROLLS

A Tale of Two Chinas

Despite all the warnings from friends and relatives, and all the pictures on TV, my homecoming visit to Guangzhou (Canton), after decades of living abroad, was an absolute eye-opener. As I stared with held breath at towering high-rises where two-story buildings once stood, I couldn't stop wondering, Where did my China go?

When immigrants return to their birthplace, they expect to relive the lives they left behind. And when reality does not match their memories, they tend to feel disheartened. The truth is, today's China is in transition: it's an ancient agrarian culture transforming into a modern industrial society. Yet, its progress is not even, neither geographically nor socially. And that's why China is a country of extreme contrasts.

Driving along the superhighway from the airport to downtown Beijing, you see a modern city skyline interrupted by an ancient Drum Tower that has stood sentry since the Ming Dynasty. But just look a little harder, however, behind the city's state-of-the-art skyscrapers, and you'll find a traditional neighborhood, a *Hutong*. Setting foot there is like stepping into the past. Instead of chain supermarkets and burger franchises, you'll find street vendors hawking fresh produce and little, mom-and-pop eateries, handed down for four or five generations.

You can see the same contrasting scenes all over China: In Shanghai, stand on the bank of the Pu River and you will simultaneously face traditional Chinese buildings, an old, European-style district, and a city center that looks like Manhattan. In Chengdu, you might emerge from a steel and glass hotel, round a corner, and bump into a house hundreds of years old.

These contrasts are not only found in building exteriors. Within some restaurants, interior designs incorporate both the old and the new. At a fashionable spot, you might sit surrounded by Chinese antiques while enjoying innovative cuisine on a modern plate decorated with traditional calligraphy or ancient symbols. Order a classic "clay pot" dish and it may actually be created and served in an oven-safe glass bowl. Time-honored cooking techniques have not been discarded, but streamlined by modern appliances that make classic dishes easier to prepare and more available. Everywhere, the old and the new Chinas are sharing the same space.

Will my "old China" fade away, eventually? I would imagine so . . . just as in the West, where there's no more horse-drawn buggies and gaslights, all civilizations must march on with time. But I am optimistic that China will find a path to the future without sacrificing her rich history and culture.

In the meantime, I am glad that the old China I remember is still there. It's alive and well, with all the wonderful aromas and noise. It's just a few blocks off the six-lane highway, still a few decades back in time.

Pan-Seared Steak Rolls

Not all great things in China are five thousand years old. This dish is a prime example—it embodies the spirit and style of modern China. This is the signature dish of Tian Di Yi Jia Restaurant in Beijing. Chef Lai developed this recipe, and he's very proud of it. You can enhance his pride by serving it to all your friends.

8 ounces flank steak, 4-inch by 6-inch piece

MARINADE

1 tbsp. soy sauce

1 tsp. vegetable oil

⅛ tsp. ground white pepper

SAUCE

1 tbsp. oyster-flavored sauce

1 tbsp. Chinese rice wine or dry sherry

2 cloves garlic, thinly sliced

¼ cup Rich Homemade Broth (page 49) or canned chicken broth

FILLING

1 tbsp. vegetable oil

1 tsp. minced garlic

1 tsp. minced ginger

1 carrot, cut into thin 1½-inch strips

½ red bell pepper, seeded and cut into thin 1½-inch strips

2 ribs celery, thinly sliced on the diagonal

1 tbsp. soy sauce

1 tsp. sesame oil

12 chives, halved crosswise

4 ounces enoki mushrooms

1 tbsp. vegetable oil

1 tbsp. butter

¼ tsp. white sesame seeds

¼ tsp. black sesame seeds

To prepare the meat, freeze the steak for 30 minutes, until partially frozen. Using a sharp knife, cut the meat against the grain, on the diagonal, into 4 equally thin slices. Use a meat mallet to pound each piece of meat to ⅛ inch thick.

To make the marinade, combine the soy sauce, oil, and white pepper in a medium bowl and mix well. Add the beef and stir to coat evenly. Let stand for 1 to 2 hours.

To make the sauce, combine the oyster sauce, wine, garlic, and broth in a small bowl and mix well.

To prepare the filling, place a wok or stir-fry pan over high heat. Add the vegetable oil, swirling to coat the sides. Add the garlic and ginger and cook, stirring, until fragrant, about 20 seconds. Add the carrot, bell pepper, and celery and stir-fry for 2 minutes. Add the soy sauce and sesame oil and stir to combine. Transfer to a bowl and let cool.

To make the beef rolls, lay the beef slices out on a work surface with the short side of each piece facing you. Equally divide the chives, enoki mushrooms, and vegetable mixture among the pieces of meat. Starting with the end closest to you, roll the beef up and over the filling, securing the seam shut with a toothpick.

Place a large skillet over medium-high heat. Add the vegetable oil and butter, swirling to coat the bottom. Add the beef rolls and pan-fry until browned on all sides, about 2 minutes. Add the sauce to the pan. Cover and simmer over medium heat until the beef is just cooked through, 3 to 4 minutes.

Transfer the rolls to a serving platter. Spoon the sauce over the rolls. Sprinkle the sesame seeds over the rolls, and serve.

MAKES 4 SERVINGS

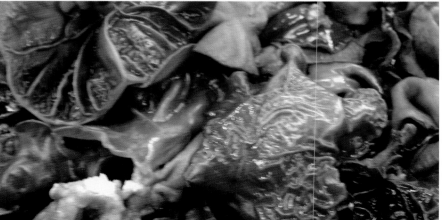

ARE MUSHROOMS GOOD LISTENERS?

In China, the most common mushrooms are black, shiitake, enoki, snow, straw, wood ear, and cloud ear mushrooms. Wood ears are fungi that grow on trees.

Chinese chefs savor mushrooms for their culinary as well as medicinal qualities. In Yunnan Province alone, there are well over one hundred different varieties of mushrooms. Many of them are sold in local open-air farmers' markets—easily the most convenient place to pick wild mushrooms.

Lucky Duck Daikon Salad

....

The next time you visit Shanghai, don't miss the fabulous T8 Restaurant in Xintiandi, the city's ultra-chic shopping and dining enclave. With innovation as one of their key objectives, restaurants such as T8 are putting Shanghai on the world's culinary map. I developed this salad in honor of a great meal we had at T8 during our last visit. This is an extremely flexible recipe. You can use whatever you have on hand: napa cabbage, cilantro, mint, or even green papaya.

DRESSING

3 tbsp. vegetable oil

3 tbsp. rice vinegar

½ tsp. minced garlic

¼ tsp. minced ginger

½ tsp. salt

2 tsp. sugar

¼ tsp. ground white pepper

1 pound daikon or jicama, cut into long, thin shreds

¼ cup shredded carrot

¼ small red onion, thinly sliced

1 green onion, green part only, julienned

SAUCE

¼ cup water

2 tbsp. hoisin sauce

2 tbsp. plum sauce

½ tsp. minced garlic

4 Preserved Duck Legs (page 65)

....

To make the dressing, whisk the oil, vinegar, garlic, ginger, salt, sugar, and white pepper together in a large bowl until the sugar dissolves. Add the daikon, carrot, red onion, and green onion and set aside to marinate for 10 minutes.

To make the sauce, combine the water, hoisin sauce, plum sauce, and garlic in a medium bowl until well mixed. Set aside.

Remove the duck meat from the bones. Use 2 forks or your fingers to finely shred the meat. Transfer the duck to the bowl with the sauce and mix well.

Arrange the salad in a mound on a serving plate. Top with the duck and serve.

MAKES 4 SERVINGS

Sweet Vinegar Peanuts

Despite its diminutive size, the peanut has an important place in the Chinese kitchen. It is both a popular staple and the source of the most common cooking oil in China. Two more interesting facts about our little peanut friend: Technically, it isn't a nut, but a legume. Also, although they are now cultivated throughout Asia, peanuts were originally introduced to China from the New World, four centuries ago. Whatever world you're in, peanuts make a wonderful snack and can be added to stir-fries and sweets or ground for use in dressings, sauces, and soups.

2 cups Virginia peanuts

SYRUP

½ cup chopped cilantro leaves

1 tsp. chopped mint leaves

6 tbsp. Chinese black vinegar or balsamic vinegar

3 tbsp. packed brown sugar

1 tsp. salt

1 tsp. toasted sesame seeds (optional)

Preheat the oven to 400 degrees F. Arrange the peanuts in a single layer on a baking sheet. Roast until the skins are lightly toasted, about 10 minutes. Remove from the oven and transfer to a bowl. Set aside.

To prepare the syrup, combine the cilantro, mint, vinegar, brown sugar, salt, and sesame seeds, if using, in a small saucepan and bring to a boil over high heat. Reduce the heat to medium-low and simmer, stirring occasionally, until the liquid is syrupy and reduced by half, about 7 minutes.

Pour the syrup over the peanuts and stir to coat evenly. Serve warm or at room temperature.

MAKES 2 CUPS

Martin Cristo

Of all the riches that the legendary Count of Monte Cristo possessed, the one we remember most was his fried ham-and-cheese sandwich. In Dali, China, the natives favor yak cheese and bread. I borrowed this idea and made it my own by encrusting the outside of the sandwich with sesame seeds and tucking a little spicy mustard and ham inside. Voila—the Martin Cristo! Since yak cheese isn't widely available (how many yaks have you seen in Wisconsin?), I chose pecorino for its gaminess.

4 slices multigrain bread	2 thin slices baked ham	2 tbsp. vegetable oil
2 tbsp. prepared Chinese hot mustard or Dijon mustard	2 eggs, beaten	1 tbsp. unsalted butter
	¼ cup milk	
2 slices (about 1 ounce each) pecorino cheese	¼ tsp. salt	
	¼ cup sesame seeds	

Lay 2 slices of the bread on a work surface, and spread each slice with some of the mustard. Top each slice with a slice of cheese and a slice of ham. Top with the remaining slices of bread. Using a sharp knife, cut the crusts off of each sandwich. (This helps to seal the edges.)

Whisk the eggs, milk, and salt together in a wide, shallow bowl. Place the sesame seeds in a second wide, shallow bowl.

Place a large, nonstick skillet over medium-high heat. Add the oil and butter, swirling to coat the bottom. Dip each sandwich into the egg mixture, drain briefly, then dip into the sesame seeds, lightly pressing the seeds into the egg and bread. Fry the sandwiches until golden and crisp, turning once, about 2 minutes per side. Cut them into halves or quarters.

Transfer the sandwiches to a serving plate and serve.

MAKES 2 SANDWICHES

Tea-Infused Chicken Kebabs

In most parts of China, grilling is not a common method of home cooking. So imagine my surprise when I discovered Xian's huge open-air food court, where, especially on an average night, 20,000 customers are served! For this recipe, I use a brining solution (salt and water) with tea to make the chicken moist and aromatic.

BRINE

2 tbsp. salt

¼ cup sugar

2-inch piece ginger, peeled and sliced into rounds

6 cloves garlic, peeled and lightly crushed

5 cups water

½ cup jasmine tea leaves

3 boneless, skinless chicken breast halves, cut into ½-inch-wide strips

2 tbsp. vegetable oil

SAUCE

¼ cup Chinese black vinegar or balsamic vinegar

¼ cup sugar

To make the brine, bring the salt, sugar, ginger, garlic, and water to a boil in a 2-quart saucepan. Meanwhile, place the tea in a large, heatproof bowl. Pour the boiling water over the tea and set aside until completely cooled, about 1 hour. Pour the tea through a fine-mesh sieve into another clean bowl, discarding the solids.

Add the chicken to the cooled tea brine, cover, and refrigerate overnight.

Soak fifteen 6-inch bamboo skewers in warm water for 30 minutes. Drain.

Drain the chicken, discarding the brine. Skewer each piece of chicken onto a bamboo skewer. Brush the skewered chicken with some of the oil.

Place a grill pan over medium-high heat until hot. Place the chicken on the grill pan and cook, turning once, until it is no longer pink in the center, about 2 minutes on each side.

Meanwhile, make the sauce. Bring the vinegar and sugar to a boil in a small saucepan over medium-high heat. Cook until the sugar dissolves.

Transfer the chicken to a serving plate. Drizzle the sauce over the top and serve.

MAKES 6 TO 8 SERVINGS

Shrimp Tulips

Peppers and eggplants are the traditional favorite "reservoirs" for stuffing vegetables. I think it's time for new recruits. When stuffed with shrimp mousse, Shanghai baby bok choy resembles a little tulip. How's that for edible art in 3-D? For yet another variation, try stuffing bitter melons. That's a classic ingredient and an all-time favorite on the Chinese menu.

12 Shanghai baby bok choy

2 tbsp. cornstarch

1 cup Shrimp Mousse (page 64), chilled

SAUCE

½ cup bottled clam juice

½ tsp. oyster-flavored sauce

¼ tsp. chili garlic sauce

⅛ tsp. ground white pepper

1 tsp. cornstarch dissolved in 2 tsp. water

3 tbsp. fish roe (optional)

Remove the outer layer of leaves from each head of bok choy. Trim each head to within 1½ inches from the root end, creating a tulip shape. Save the leaves and trimmings for Ginger-Garlic Baby Bok Choy (page 106). Cut the root end of each tulip so that it sits upright, root side down. To shape the petals, use a paring knife to cut a V into each leaf (each tulip should have about 3 petals). Use a small melon baller to scoop out the core of each tulip.

Prepare a wok or stir-fry pan for steaming (see page 23). Lightly dust each tulip with cornstarch, shaking off the excess. Fill each with a rounded tbsp. of the shrimp mousse, using a wet finger to smooth the top of the mousse. Arrange the filled bok choy, root side down, in the steamer. Cover and steam over high heat until the shrimp mousse is just cooked through, about 6 minutes.

Meanwhile, make the sauce. Put the clam juice, oyster sauce, chili garlic sauce, and white pepper in a small saucepan. Bring to a boil over medium-high heat. Add the cornstarch mixture and cook, stirring, until the sauce boils and thickens.

Transfer the bok choy to a serving plate. Garnish each with fish roe, if desired. Spoon the sauce around the plate and serve.

MAKES 4 TO 6 SERVINGS

Yin-Yang Vegetable Pockets

This dish truly represents the principles of yin and yang. The textural differences provide a balance of crisp and delicate, crunchy and soft, pan-fried and steamed. For a heartier filling, add half a pound of cooked ground meat with the vegetables.

FILLING

1 tbsp. plus 1 tsp. vegetable oil

1 tsp. minced garlic

1 cup shredded napa cabbage

½ cup shredded carrot

½ cup yellow chives, cut into 1-inch-long pieces, or bean sprouts

¼ cup shredded red onion

1 tbsp. oyster-flavored sauce

1 tsp. sesame oil

3 eggs, beaten

¼ tsp. salt

⅛ tsp. ground white pepper

20 to 24 round pot sticker wrappers

1 egg, beaten with 1 tbsp. water

2 cups plus 2 tbsp. vegetable oil

3 tbsp. rice vinegar

¼ cup water

½ cup Soy-Vinegar Dipping Sauce (page 52)

To prepare the filling, place a wok or stir-fry pan over high heat. Add 1 tbsp. of the oil, swirling to coat the sides. Add the garlic and cook, stirring, until fragrant, about 10 seconds. Add the cabbage, carrot, chives, and red onion and stir-fry until the vegetables are tender-crisp, about 2 minutes. Add the oyster-flavored sauce and sesame oil and toss to coat. Transfer the vegetable mixture to a colander to drain. Set aside in a medium bowl.

Place a medium nonstick skillet over medium-high heat until hot. Add the remaining 1 tsp. oil, swirling to coat the bottom. Pour the eggs into the pan, tilting the pan so the egg coats the bottom, and cook until the bottom of the omelet is set, about 1 minute. Season with the salt and pepper. Turn the omelet and cook until the second side is just set, about 30 seconds. Slide the omelet onto a cutting board. Fold in half and cut into thin shreds. Transfer to the bowl of vegetables and set aside until cool.

To form the dumplings, place 1 pot sticker wrapper on a clean, flat surface, keeping the remaining wrappers covered with a damp kitchen towel to prevent them from drying out. Place 2 heaping tbsp. of filling in the center of the wrapper. Moisten the edges of the wrapper with the egg wash. Top with a second wrapper and secure the edges. Starting from one end of the wrapper, slightly fold over the edge (like a pie crust) and continue folding around the dumpling. Repeat this process with the remaining wrappers and filling. Keep the dumplings covered with a damp kitchen towel to prevent them from drying out.

RECIPE CONTINUES ON NEXT PAGE

For the Yin dumplings, heat 2 tbsp. of the oil in a large, nonstick skillet over medium-high heat. Add half of the filled dumplings, flat side down, and cook, without turning, until golden brown, about 3 minutes. Add the vinegar and water. Reduce the heat to medium, cover, and steam until the dumplings are tender, about 4 minutes.

For the Yang dumplings, heat the remaining 2 cups oil in a wok or stir-fry pan over medium-high heat until hot. Working with a few at a time, add the remaining uncooked dumplings and shallow-fry, turning once, until golden brown and crisp, about 2 minutes per side. Lift the dumplings out with a wire strainer or slotted spoon and drain on paper towels.

Transfer the Yin and Yang dumplings to a serving plate. Serve with the dipping sauce on the side.

MAKES 10 TO 12 DUMPLINGS

A BIT OF YIN, A BIT OF YANG, A BIT OF YAN

In Chinese philosophy, the universe operates as two opposing but complementary principles: "yang," meaning fire, light, and dominance, and "yin," meaning air, water, and submission. The dominance of one over the other creates health or financial problems. One way to restore harmony is through diet. For instance, eating only proteins and deep-fried foods creates too much yang. Cool down with vegetables, fruits, and water.

When balanced, these principles coexist productively: Yang creates ideas and yin produces material forms. I've given you the yang—great recipe ideas. Now you supply the yin—go make them!

Lamb Siu Mai with Spicy Tomato Sauce

Siu mai are popular dim sum dumplings from Cantonese teahouses. Usually made of pork and shrimp, this Northern Chinese twist uses lamb instead. Spicy tomato sauce complements the lamb's strong flavors.

FILLING

8 ounces ground lamb

2 whole water chestnuts, minced

2 tsp. Chinese rice wine or dry sherry

2 tsp. oyster-flavored sauce

1 tsp. cornstarch

12 square wonton wrappers

SAUCE

2 tbsp. vegetable oil

1 tbsp. minced garlic

1 tbsp. minced ginger

2 tomatoes, peeled and chopped

¼ cup Rich Homemade Broth (page 49) or canned chicken broth

1 tsp. chili garlic sauce

1 tsp. soy sauce

1 tsp. sesame oil

1 tsp. cornstarch dissolved in 2 tsp. water

2 lettuce leaves

1 tbsp. chopped cilantro

1 green onion, chopped

To make the filling, combine the ground lamb, water chestnuts, rice wine, oyster sauce, and cornstarch in a bowl until well mixed.

To make the dumplings, place a heaping tsp. of filling in the center of a wonton wrapper. (Keep the remaining wrappers covered with a damp towel to prevent them from drying.) Bring the sides of the wrapper together, bunching them around the filling and smoothing any pleats. Flatten the bottom of the dumpling by tapping it against a flat surface, and squeeze the sides of the dumpling gently so the filling plumps out of the top. Keep the formed dumplings covered with a damp towel to prevent them from drying.

To make the sauce, heat a wok or stir-fry pan over high heat until hot. Add the oil, swirling to coat the sides. Add the garlic and ginger. Cook, stirring, until fragrant, about 10 seconds. Add the tomatoes and stir-fry until the excess liquid is evaporated, 3 to 4 minutes. Add the broth, chili garlic sauce, soy sauce, and sesame oil. Bring to a boil. Add the cornstarch mixture and cook, stirring, until the sauce boils and thickens, about 1 minute. Keep the sauce warm over low heat.

Prepare a wok or stir-fry pan for steaming (see page 23). Line a steaming basket with the lettuce leaves. Arrange the dumplings, without them touching one another, in the prepared basket. Cover and steam over high heat until the filling is cooked through, 4 to 5 minutes.

Pour the sauce onto a serving plate. Arrange the *siu mai* on top of the sauce. Sprinkle the cilantro and green onion on top and serve.

MAKES 12 DUMPLINGS, ABOUT 4 SERVINGS

TOUCH THE HEART

After feasting on *dim sum* (touch the heart), you'll appreciate its name! This small-plate cuisine can be traced to ancient teahouses along the Silk Road. Following an imperial physician's dictum to never ingest tea with food, teahouses originally offered weary merchants and farmers only tea.

When tea later became known as a digestive aid, enterprising teahouse operators began serving snacks. During the tenth-century Sung Dynasty, the art of dim sum flourished, with chefs creating more than a thousand tasty little dishes to accompany tea. And the classic Chinese brunch was born!

Mushroom Medley Soup

China's Yunnan Province is famous for its legendary variety of mushrooms. I was tempted to name this recipe Martin Yan's All-Star Mushroom Soup. I had a tough time selecting the mushrooms for this recipe, because there are just so many to choose from. Next time you visit Yunnan, ask the natives to take you on a mushroom harvest hike. It's great exercise for your legs and a fantastic treat for your taste buds.

3 cups fresh mushrooms, such as button, porto-bello, shiitake, and/or oyster

2 tbsp. vegetable oil

1 tbsp. butter

1 tbsp. minced ginger

2 ribs celery, chopped

One 12-ounce can whole straw mushrooms, drained

2 tbsp. oyster-flavored sauce

4 cups Rich Homemade Broth (page 49) or canned chicken broth

1 cup half-and-half

3 tbsp. soy sauce

¼ tsp. ground black pepper

Chili Oil (page 58) or a store-bought version for garnish

Cilantro Oil (page 58) for garnish

If using button mushrooms, thinly slice them. If using portobello or shiitake mushrooms, remove and discard the stems and slice the caps. If using oyster mushrooms, trim off the woody root ends.

Place a wok, stir-fry pan, or medium pot over medium-high heat. Add the oil and butter, swirling to coat the sides. Add the ginger and celery and cook, stirring, until the ginger is fragrant, about 30 seconds. Add the fresh mushrooms and straw mushrooms and stir-fry until the mushrooms begin to give off some of their liquid, 3 to 4 minutes. Add the oyster sauce and stir to coat. Add the broth and bring to a boil. Reduce the heat to medium-low, cover, and simmer for 10 minutes.

Add the half-and-half and soy sauce and return to a boil. Season with the pepper and simmer for 5 minutes more. Working in batches, purée the soup in a blender. Return the soup to the pan over medium-high heat and cook until hot.

Ladle the soup into bowls. Garnish each with a few drops of chili oil and cilantro oil, and serve.

MAKES 4 SERVINGS

Mom's Chicken Soup

Every mother in the world has her favorite chicken soup. My mom put her faith in black chicken—known for its medicinal quality—and ginkgo nuts. I am adapting this recipe to suit our local market ingredients, and substituting Cornish game hens for black chicken.

2 Cornish game hens or one
3- to 4-pound whole chicken

6 dried black mushrooms

6 thick slices ginger, crushed

2 cloves garlic, crushed

8 ounces thawed frozen
ginkgo nuts or drained canned
garbanzo beans

1 tbsp. dried wolfberries
(optional)

1 cup Chinese rice wine
or dry sherry

2 tbsp. soy sauce

2 tsp. salt

1 tsp. ground white pepper

Bring a medium pot of water to a boil over high heat. Add the game hens, return to a boil, and boil for 5 minutes. Lift the hens from the pot and set aside. Discard the cooking liquid.

In a small bowl, soak the mushrooms in warm water to cover until softened, about 15 minutes; drain. Discard the stems, quarter the caps, and set aside.

Return the clean pot to the stove top. Add the hens, ginger, and garlic and enough water to just cover, 8 to 10 cups. Bring to a boil over high heat. Add the ginkgo nuts, wolfberries (if using), mushrooms, wine, soy sauce, salt, and white pepper. Reduce the heat to medium and simmer, partially covered, until the hens are cooked through, about 1 hour.

Using a wire strainer or slotted spoon, remove hens, straining briefly, to cutting board. Cut each hen in half lengthwise. Place each half into serving bowls. Ladle the soup into bowls and serve.

MAKES 4 SERVINGS

BERRY NUTTY FOR NUTS & BERRIES

Ginkgo nuts are not really nuts, and wolfberries are not berries for wolves. Called *bai gu*, ginkgo nuts are actually the seeds of the fruit of the maidenhair tree. Proven blood thinners, they're also thought to fortify cells and improve mental alertness

Wolfberries, long used by the Chinese to fight infection, improve eyesight, and protect the liver, have gained worldwide recognition for their nutrients, especially lutein, and their antioxidant qualities. The Chinese eat them dried, as juice, or in soups, congees, wine, and tea. You can even enjoy a pint of wolfberry beer!

Golden Curry Pumpkin Soup

Chinese cooks use pumpkin and squash in a variety of dishes, including soup. The soy sauce in this recipe enhances the flavor of the pumpkin and gives the soup a rich golden color, while the curry adds an extra roundness to the texture.

8 cups peeled, cubed butternut squash or other firm winter squash

4 cups Rich Homemade Broth (page 49) or canned chicken broth

1 tbsp. minced ginger

2 tsp. minced garlic

1 tbsp. yellow curry powder or red curry paste

1 tbsp. pine nuts

½ cup unsweetened coconut milk

2 tbsp. soy sauce

1 tsp. salt

¼ tsp. ground white pepper

8 ounces soft tofu, drained and diced

1 green onion, chopped

In a medium pot, combine the squash, broth, ginger, and garlic. Bring to a boil over high heat, reduce the heat to low, and simmer uncovered until the squash is very tender, about 1 hour. Add the curry powder or paste and stir to incorporate.

In a small frying pan, toast the pine nuts over medium heat, shaking the pan frequently, until lightly colored, about 5 minutes. Immediately pour onto a plate to cool.

Working in batches, purée the squash and broth in a blender. Return the purée to the pot. Add the coconut milk, soy sauce, salt, and white pepper and bring to a boil over medium-high heat. Stir in the tofu and simmer until heated through.

Ladle the soup into bowls. Garnish each bowl with pine nuts and green onion and serve.

MAKES 6 TO 8 SERVINGS

Fortune Noodle Meatball Soup

Soup is the ultimate comfort food, and this is the ultimate soup. I love this soup on a cold, wintry day. It has everything I like: meatballs, noodles, and a hot-and-sour broth. Wood ears are black fungi that grow on trees. Other members in this family are cloud ears and snow ears. With so many ears, trees must be great listeners!

2 ounces dried wood ear mushrooms

3 ounces fresh Chinese wheat noodles or dried spaghetti

MEATBALLS

1 pound ground meat

1 tbsp. cornstarch

2 tsp. sesame oil

2½ tsp. salt

½ tsp. ground white pepper

4 cups Rich Homemade Broth (page 49) or canned chicken broth

3 tbsp. Chinese black vinegar or balsamic vinegar

2 tbsp. diced pickled mustard greens

1 tsp. salt

Pinch of ground white pepper

2 green onions, thinly sliced

3 sprigs cilantro, both leaves and stems, minced

1 tbsp. Chili Oil (page 58) or a store-bought version

In a bowl, soak the mushrooms in warm water to cover until softened, about 15 minutes. Drain. Thinly slice the mushrooms and set aside.

Bring a medium-sized pot filled with water to a boil over high heat. Add the noodles and cook according to the package directions. Drain, rinse with warm water, and drain again. Place the noodles in a bowl and cover to keep warm.

To prepare the meatballs, put the meat, cornstarch, sesame oil, salt, and pepper in a food processor and process to a smooth paste. Scoop the meatball mixture out into a medium bowl. With wet hands, roll the mixture into walnut-sized balls, using a heaping tbsp. for each ball. Arrange the meatballs, without crowding, on a lightly greased plate.

To make the soup, in a medium pot, combine the broth and vinegar and bring to a boil over high heat. Add the meatballs and return to a boil. Reduce the heat to medium and simmer until the meatballs are cooked through, about 8 minutes. Stir in the mushrooms and pickled greens and simmer for 2 minutes more. Add the cooked noodles and cook, stirring, until the noodles are heated through. Season to taste with salt and pepper.

Ladle the soup into bowls. Garnish each bowl with some of the green onions, cilantro, and chili oil, and serve.

MAKES 6 SERVINGS

Vegetables

Favorable geographical and climatic conditions in Southern China have made this region the country's rice and vegetable basket. Back in Guangzhou, my mom would go to the farmers' market each morning to pick out the freshest vegetables. I often accompanied her, helping by dragging along a wicker shopping basket that must have been as wide as I was tall.

Back then, the Chinese diet was made up of more vegetable fiber than animal protein. Once again, geography was a contributing factor. With a large population and limited acreage available for raising cattle and livestock, beef was expensive, and even pork and chicken were considered treats. My mother never had to remind us to "eat our vegetables," because oftentimes that was all we had on the dinner table!

Looking back, I think that our hardship had a silver lining. They say "Necessity is the mother of invention." Well, Chinese chefs are among the world's most inventive minds when it comes to incorporating vegetables into their menus and developing ingenious recipes for them. And as health experts are now discovering, a diet rich in vegetables offers great advantages, so my early quasi-vegetarian regimen actually provided me a healthy start in life.

What is the state of vegetables in today's industrialized and more prosperous China? In my recent visits, I did notice that the country's economic gains and recent technological advances have changed the look of the home dinner table. There is a greater variety of dishes and, yes, more meat, poultry, and seafood.

But chefs all over China still show tremendous passion for creating new vegetable dishes, or reinventing classical ones. A good example is Rainbow Stir-Fry (page 116). It's my homage to the Shanxi classic *chao bu lan*—a stir-fry dish made mostly of shredded potato dusted with flour. In the old days, it was a common dish for poor working families. These days, the same dish is dressed up and served in many fine restaurants in Shanxi.

For those of you who have a problem convincing your kids to eat their vegetables, here's my advice: Don't tell, show! Put the recipes in this chapter to good use and show your kids that vegetables are not only good for them, they are just . . . good.

Braised Mushroom Trio

Why settle for one kind of mushroom when you can have three? This is a dream dish for mushroom lovers. You can use Chinese dried mushrooms if fresh ones are unavailable. If using dried, soak the whole mushrooms in hot water for at least 20 minutes before proceeding. Don't waste the flavorful soaking liquid. Pour it through a coffee filter or fine-mesh strainer and save it to use in sauces, soups, and stews.

SAUCE

½ cup Rich Homemade Broth (page 49) or canned chicken broth

¼ cup water

2 tbsp. oyster-flavored sauce

2 tbsp. soy sauce

1½ tsp. packed light brown sugar

4 ounces broccoli florets (about 3 cups)

Salt

1 tbsp. vegetable oil

2 cloves garlic, crushed

2 quarter-sized slices ginger, crushed

4 baby portobello mushrooms, gills removed

4 shiitake mushrooms, stemmed

4 large white mushrooms, stemmed

1 tsp. cornstarch dissolved in 2 tsp. water

To make the sauce, combine the broth, water, oyster sauce, soy sauce, and brown sugar in a small bowl and mix well. Set aside.

To prepare the broccoli, bring a 2-quart pan filled with water to a boil over high heat. Add the broccoli and cook until bright green and tender-crisp, about 1 minute. Drain, rinse with cold water, and drain again. Set aside.

Place a wok or stir-fry pan over high heat. Add the oil, swirling to coat the sides. Add the garlic and ginger and cook, stirring, until fragrant, about 10 seconds. Add the mushrooms and stir-fry until the caps begin to brown, about 1 minute. Add the sauce and stir to coat. Cover and cook until the mushrooms are tender, about 8 minutes. Add the cornstarch mixture and cook, stirring, until the sauce boils and thickens.

Arrange the broccoli in the center of a serving plate and arrange the mushrooms around it. Pour the sauce over all and serve.

MAKES 4 SERVINGS

Corn Stir-Fry

No doubt about it, we are definitely getting cornier. Pressed tofu is made by pressing tofu in a dark, savory marinade, and it can be found in most Asian and health-food markets. Originally a Western import, corn has found a place at the Chinese dining table, like other New World veggies, such as tomatoes and eggplants. These days, corn is cultivated and consumed regularly in many parts of China and complements pressed tofu.

3 ears fresh corn, shucked, or 2 cups thawed frozen corn kernels

½ tsp. whole Sichuan peppercorns

2 tbsp. vegetable oil

1 tomato, cored and diced

½ red bell pepper, diced

¼ cup diced onion

¼ cup peeled, diced jicama

¼ cup diced pressed or baked tofu

3 tbsp. chopped water chestnuts

1 tbsp. soy sauce

½ tsp. salt

¼ tsp. sugar

3 sprigs cilantro, both leaves and stems, chopped

If using fresh corn, shave the kernels off each ear with a sharp knife. Transfer to a medium bowl and set aside.

In a small frying pan, toast the Sichuan peppercorns over medium heat, shaking the pan frequently, until fragrant and lightly toasted, 1 to 2 minutes. Immediately pour them onto a plate to cool.

Place a wok or stir-fry pan over medium-high heat. Add the oil, swirling to coat the sides. Add the corn, tomato, bell pepper, onion, jicama, tofu, and water chestnuts and stir-fry until the vegetables are tender-crisp, about 2 minutes. Add the soy sauce, salt, sugar, and Sichuan peppercorns, tossing until well combined.

Transfer to a serving plate, garnish with the cilantro, and serve.

MAKES 4 SERVINGS

Ginger-Garlic Baby Bok Choy

....

On my last trip to Shanghai, I noticed that baby bok choy was served with practically every meal. Those who are familiar with the wonderful taste and texture of this leafy vegetable will need no convincing to make this dish. By the way, this is a great way to use up the tops of the bok choy left over from making Shrimp Tulips (page 86). For a change of pace (and taste), you might try the same recipe using Chinese broccoli (*gai lan*), water spinach (*oong choy*), or mature pea shoots (*do miu*) instead.

1 pound baby bok choy, halved lengthwise

SAUCE

2 tbsp. Chinese rice wine or dry sherry

2 tsp. oyster-flavored sauce

1 tsp. soy sauce

¼ tsp. salt

⅛ tsp. ground black pepper

1 tbsp. vegetable oil

1 tbsp. minced garlic

1 tbsp. minced ginger

....

Blanch the bok choy in a large pot of salted water until bright green, about 1 minute. Drain, rinse with cold water, and drain again. Set aside.

To make the sauce, combine the wine, oyster sauce, soy sauce, salt, and pepper in a small bowl and mix well.

Heat a wok or stir-fry pan over high heat until hot. Add the oil, swirling to coat the sides. Add the garlic and ginger and cook, stirring, until fragrant, about 10 seconds. Add the bok choy and sauce and stir-fry until the liquid has reduced by half, 1 to 2 minutes.

Transfer to a serving plate and serve.

MAKES 4 SERVINGS

Yellow Chive Omelet

This was one of my favorite dishes when I was a boy. It's so simple, and so easy to make. Chinese yellow chives have a distinctive, subtle flavor that you can't get anywhere else. If you can't find yellow chives, use green chives, garlic chives, or green onions. To make things more exciting, I mix in a bit of chili sauce. You can use XO sauce in place of the chili sauce.

6 eggs, beaten

¼ cup bean sprouts

¼ cup grated carrot

¼ cup sliced yellow onion

1 green onion, green part only, thinly sliced

½ tsp. salt

⅛ tsp. ground white pepper

2 tbsp. vegetable oil

4 ounces fresh Chinese yellow chives, cut into ½-inch lengths

2 tsp. Chef Yan's Chili Sauce (page 56) or store-bought XO sauce

In a medium bowl, whisk the eggs, bean sprouts, carrot, yellow onion, green onion, salt, and white pepper together.

Heat an 8- or 9-inch nonstick frying pan over medium heat until hot. Add the oil, swirling to coat the bottom. Add the chives and cook, stirring, until softened, about 1 minute. Pour the egg mixture into the pan. Cook, without stirring, until the edges begin to set, about 2 minutes. Lift with a spatula and shake or tilt the pan to let the uncooked egg flow beneath. Continue to cook until the egg no longer flows freely, about 2 minutes more. Turn the omelet over and brown lightly on the other side.

Slide the omelet onto a clean cutting board and cut into 8 wedges. Transfer to a serving plate, drizzle with the chili sauce, and serve.

MAKES 4 SERVINGS

Dry-Fried Green Beans

Green beans have had a rough time in North America. For generations, they have had the misfortune of being overcooked and served bland and mushy. That's not the case with this dish. The oil-blanching seals in the moisture and freshness, and the quick dry-frying adds that special wok "aroma." I also like to use Chinese yard-long beans for this recipe. Choose smaller or younger beans that have a lighter shade of green and are more flexible.

SAUCE

¼ cup Rich Homemade Broth (page 49) or canned chicken broth

1 tbsp. soy sauce

2 tsp. minced garlic

2 tsp. chili garlic sauce

¼ tsp. sesame oil

2 tsp. sugar

½ tsp. salt

2 cups vegetable oil

¾ pound green beans, ends trimmed, cut into 2-inch lengths

½ tsp. cornstarch dissolved in 1 tsp. water

To make the sauce, combine the broth, soy sauce, garlic, chili garlic sauce, sesame oil, sugar, and salt in a bowl and stir until well mixed.

Pour the oil into a 2-quart saucepan and heat to 350 degrees F over medium-high heat. Carefully slip the green beans into the oil and cook, stirring continuously, until they are wrinkled, about 1 minute. With a slotted spoon or wire skimmer, transfer the beans to paper towels to drain. Reserve the oil.

Heat a wok or stir-fry pan over high heat until hot. Add 2 tsp. of the reserved oil, swirling to coat the sides. Discard any remaining oil, or strain and save for another use. Add the green beans and sauce and stir-fry until the sauce boils. Add the cornstarch mixture and cook until the sauce thickens.

Transfer to a serving plate and serve.

MAKES 4 SERVINGS

Steamed Tofu
with Black Bean Sauce

I've heard the complaint countless times: tofu is too bland. Instead of seeing it as a flaw, however, I see it as a strength. The neutrality of tofu makes it the perfect food to absorb other flavors, especially strong ones, like salted black beans, which lend a distinctly pungent, smoky flavor to this recipe. Serve this dish with steamed brown rice for a truly tasty and healthy meal.

SAUCE

1 tbsp. Black Bean Sauce (page 41) or a store-bought version

1 tbsp. soy sauce

1 tsp. sesame oil

2 tsp. sugar

One 16-ounce package soft tofu, drained

1 green onion, julienned

3 sprigs cilantro

1 small red bird chile, sliced on the diagonal, leaving the seeds in for heat (optional)

1 tbsp. vegetable oil

To make the sauce, combine the black bean sauce, soy sauce, sesame oil, and sugar in a small bowl and stir until the sugar dissolves.

Cut the tofu widthwise into 8 equal slices. Carefully transfer the tofu to a heatproof glass dish that will fit into your steamer comfortably.

Prepare a wok or stir-fry pan for steaming (see page 23). Steam the tofu, covered, until heated through, about 2 minutes. Pour the sauce over the top and steam for another 2 minutes. Garnish with the green onion, cilantro, and sliced chile, if using.

In a small saucepan, heat the vegetable oil to almost smoking and drizzle it over the top of the dish. Serve immediately.

MAKES 4 SERVINGS

Pea Shoots with Soft Tofu

Fans of contrasting textures will be on sensory overdrive with this dish. It combines the amazing tender flavor of mature pea shoots with the smooth texture of soft tofu. You can find fresh young or mature pea shoots in many Asian and health-food markets. On Western menus, young pea shoots are often served in salads. You will be a fan in no time.

SAUCE

⅓ cup Rich Homemade Broth (page 49) or canned chicken or vegetable broth

2 tbsp. vegetarian stir-fry sauce or oyster-flavored sauce

1 tbsp. Chinese rice wine or dry sherry

1 tsp. soy sauce

1 tsp. sugar

1 pound soft tofu, drained

1 tbsp. vegetable oil

½ tsp. minced ginger

1 tsp. minced garlic

4 cups fresh mature pea shoots

1 tsp. cornstarch dissolved in 2 tsp. water

To make the sauce, combine the broth, stir-fry sauce, wine, soy sauce, and sugar in a small bowl, stirring until the sugar dissolves.

Cut the tofu into 1½-inch cubes.

Heat a wok or stir-fry pan over high heat until hot. Add the oil, swirling to coat the sides. Add the ginger and garlic and cook, stirring, until fragrant, about 10 seconds. Add the pea shoots and stir-fry until they just begin to wilt, about 1 minute. Add the sauce and bring to a boil. Add the cornstarch mixture and cook, stirring, until the sauce thickens slightly. Add the tofu and cook until heated through.

Transfer to a serving plate and serve.

MAKES 4 SERVINGS

TOFU FOR YOU!

Tofu is as exciting to a Chinese chef as a blank canvas is to an artist. Its versatility, variety of textures, and tendency to take on other ingredients' flavors make it perfect for soups, entrées, drinks, and desserts. Scoop out the center, and it becomes a pocket for savory fillings. Made of soybean milk with a coagulant, this classic Asian food is gaining popularity worldwide. With a highprotein content, B vitamins, and isoflavones, it's a nutritional powerhouse!

Watercress and Watermelon Salad

Although the Chinese love vegetables, we generally prefer them cooked. The concept of mixing a bunch of raw veggies in a bowl and calling it a meal is not an easy sell. To be honest, I was also partial to cooked vegetables until I tasted fresh, raw watercress. Growing up, I loved watercress in soup and in stir-fries, but uncooked? Never! Try it with the special dressing in this recipe, and in no time, you too will love it.

2 shallots

Vegetable oil for deep-frying

DRESSING

2 tbsp. rice vinegar

2 tbsp. vegetable oil

1 tbsp. freshly squeezed lime juice

1 tsp. minced ginger

1 tsp. soy sauce

2 bunches watercress, woody stems trimmed

1 cup julienned seedless watermelon

½ cup julienned jicama

¼ cup julienned pickled ginger

¼ cup julienned crystallized ginger

¼ cup walnuts, toasted

Peel the shallots, then thinly slice into rounds. Set aside. Pour the oil to a depth of 1½ inches in a 1-quart saucepan. Heat over medium heat until the temperature reaches 310 degrees F. Add the shallots and gently fry, stirring often, until they turn evenly golden brown and crisp, about 20 minutes. Remove the shallots with a wire strainer or slotted spoon to paper towels to drain. Set aside.

To make the dressing, whisk the vinegar, oil, lime juice, ginger, and soy sauce together in a small bowl until well mixed.

Place the watercress on a serving plate. Arrange the watermelon, jicama, pickled ginger, crystallized ginger, walnuts, and shallots over the watercress. Pour the dressing over the top and toss just before serving.

MAKES 6 SERVINGS

Rainbow Stir-Fry

Those of you who still think that all potatoes are born in Idaho need to look further across the ocean, to China. Amazing but true: Despite the popularity of its rice and noodle dishes, China is the number one producer of potatoes. For this dish, we combine shredded potatoes and other vegetables to make a comforting side dish.

2 tbsp. plus 1 tsp. vegetable oil

1 egg, beaten

1 large potato, peeled and cut into long, thin shreds

1 tbsp. chopped garlic

1 small carrot, peeled and cut into long, thin shreds

½ red onion, thinly sliced

¾ cup Rich Homemade Broth (page 49) or canned chicken broth

2 tbsp. vegetarian mushroom stir-fry sauce or oyster-flavored sauce

1 tbsp. soy sauce

¼ tsp. ground black pepper

¼ red bell pepper, seeded and cut into narrow strips

¼ green bell pepper, seeded and cut into narrow strips

2 tbsp. rice vinegar

1 tsp. sesame oil

Place a 6-inch nonstick skillet over medium-high heat until hot. Add 1 tsp. of the oil and swirl to coat the bottom. Pour the egg into the pan, tilting the pan so the egg coats the bottom, and cook until the bottom is set, about 1 minute. Turn the omelet and cook until the second side is cooked, about 30 seconds. Slide the omelet out onto a cutting board, fold it in half, and cut into thin shreds. Set aside.

Bring a 2-quart saucepan filled with water to a boil over high heat. Add the potato shreds and cook until tender-crisp, about 2 minutes. Drain well. Set aside.

Place a wok or stir-fry pan over high heat until hot. Add the remaining 2 tbsp. oil, swirling to coat the sides. Add the garlic, carrot, and red onion and cook, stirring, until the carrot softens, about 1 minute. Add the potatoes and stir-fry for 1 minute. Add the broth, stir-fry sauce, soy sauce, and black pepper and cook until the liquid is reduced by half, 2 to 3 minutes. Add the bell peppers and shredded egg and cook until heated through. Remove from the heat and add the vinegar and sesame oil, tossing until well mixed.

Transfer to a serving plate and serve hot, warm, or chilled.

MAKES 4 SERVINGS

Roots

As agrarian China transforms into an industrial powerhouse, people joke that the biggest new crop is Chinese yuppies. But while an urban business-person frets over stock reports on his computer, his rural cousin's main concern is growing enough food for his family. When you go from China's cities to the countryside, you go from the industrial revolution to a timeless world where farming reigns. On recent visits to China, I have studied food production in rural areas. Although that was my professional reason for these trips, it wasn't the only reason. I sense that, despite all the new economic advances, the soul of China, its very essence, still lies deep in the country.

Climate and geography determine the unique ingredients that each region of the country produces. In Southern China, with its warm weather, generous rainfalls, and crisscrossing waterways, produce abounds, and underwater plants, such as water chestnuts, bamboo shoots, and taro, thrive. In my grandfather's village of Kaiping, I picked green leafy vegetables like bok choy and water spinach, herded chickens and ducks, and sloshed through rice fields still tended by farmers with water buffalo.

In colder, dryer Northern China, wheat is the major crop. Instead of water buffalo, I herded cattle. Since idle hands are never tolerated, I soon found myself harvesting cabbage in the nippy air. Here farmers serve foods that would warm the heart of any American from the Midwest—turnips, carrots, pumpkins, and corn on the cob.

Outside of Shanghai and to its east flows the world's oldest and longest human-made waterway—the famous Grand Canal. The intricate water system and moderate temperatures of this area create perfect conditions for growing rice, beans, and soybeans.

Western China is saddled with cold, harsh winters and hot, humid summers. On the high plains, local farmers grow potatoes, corn, barley, and wheat. Rest assured: There will never be a potato famine here.

Sichuan Province, the "rice bowl" of China, also produces sugarcane, potatoes, fruits, wheat, corn, beets, sweet potatoes, and beans. More cattle and pigs are raised here than in any other area of the country. I also saw sheep, goats, and yaks.

The diverse topography of Yunnan Province, in farthest southwestern China, ranges from tropical rainforests to mountains. Some parts of this region are filled with orchards, a fruit-lover's paradise. During spring, the rugged mountains transform into beautiful yellow domes covered with blooming rapeseed plants, which produce canola oil. Local farmers also harvest sunflowers and export their seeds as snacks, paste fillings, and cooking oil.

Amidst the breathtaking peaks of Shangri-la, you see a lot of high mountain wheat and young city folks in their SUVs, checking out China's cool "Wild West." These harsh mountain areas also yield chicken-eye beans, used to make gelatin, noodles, and chicken-eye noodle cakes—vegetarian treats, despite their name.

The Chinese literally believe the old saying, "You are what you eat." Food plays a central role in every community's social life. And over time, the foods available in each region have contributed to its distinctive cultural and culinary characteristics. To truly understand China, you really do need to explore its "roots."

Rice &
Noodles

I admit it: I am partial to rice. As a native of Southern China, the "homeland of fish and rice," I view my bowl of steamed rice the same way most Europeans view bread on their dining table—as an essential part of the meal. When my boys were really young, they once asked me, during dinner, how many bowls of rice I had eaten in my life. I said, "I don't know, but tonight I am adding at least two more to that count." Let's see, two bowls a meal, two meals a day, plus a bowl of rice soup for breakfast—that makes, well, a lot of hours washing bowls!

I'm not alone in my devotion. My love for rice is shared by most of the population in Southern China. During a recent visit to Guangzhou, I was treated to the classic clay pot dish of Preserved Duck with Clay Pot Rice (page 124). As a child, I could sniff out that tantalizing aroma in the wintry air of a late afternoon when I was walking home from school. No matter how tired I was after a long day of classes, that unique scent would add an extra spring to my step as I made my way home.

Another special dish that would "rice" to the occasion was my grandma's version of Yang Chow fried rice. She always used leftover rice because it separates better in the wok. With so many healthy appetites in our household, leftover rice was a rarity. By the way, Yang Chow fried rice was not really created in Yang Chow but in Southern China. (See Grandma Yan's Signature Fried Rice, page 126.)

And now a few well-deserved words about noodles: I love them, too! Many people think that noodles are strictly a Northern Chinese passion. They should try a Hong Kong favorite, *liang mein huang* (Pan-Fried Noodle Cakes, page 137). They're golden crispy on the outside and tender to the bite on the inside—absolutely heavenly!

From Shanxi, the capital of noodles, I bring you not one wave of pleasure, but two in one bite. Double Happiness handmade noodles are a local specialty that noodle lovers line up for daily. The noodles for each order are handmade, often just moments before they are cooked. The noodle chefs of Shanxi are by far the handiest chefs in China.

Rice or noodles—what will it be for dinner tonight? Serve both and you won't have to worry about tomorrow's lunch!

Carrot Rice

....

This aromatic carrot rice is a perfect example of comfort food. It has the natural sweetness of carrots, a subtle spice from ginger, and all the warm satisfaction of fresh steamed rice. It's a perfect accompaniment to grilled dishes such as New Beijing Lamb (page 190) or Grilled Spiced Pork Chops (page 177).

2 cups water	1 tsp. vegetable oil
1 cup long-grain rice	½ tsp. salt
½ cup grated carrot	⅛ tsp. grated ginger

....

In a 2-quart pan, combine the water, rice, carrot, vegetable oil, salt, and ginger. Bring to a boil over high heat, reduce the heat to low, and simmer, uncovered, until craterlike holes form on the surface of the rice, about 6 minutes. Cover and continue cooking, undisturbed, until all the liquid is absorbed, about 10 minutes.

Fluff the rice with a fork. Transfer to a serving platter and serve.

MAKES 4 SERVINGS

Preserved Duck with Clay Pot Rice

There was something magical about watching puffs of white steam escape the edge of a bobbing clay pot lid! Oh, what a wonderful aroma of preserved duck filled up my mom's tiny kitchen! I love all my stainless steel pots and my state-of-the-art electric rice cooker. Yet nothing can replace my old clay pot: the way it perfumes the rice, the crunchy crust that forms on the bottom of the pot, and the savory warmth that always reminds me of a hearty winter meal.

4 dried black mushrooms

2 cups Rich Homemade Broth (page 49) or canned chicken broth

1 cup long-grain rice

1 tbsp. soy sauce

1 tsp. minced ginger

2 Preserved Duck Legs (page 65), meat removed from the bone

1 Chinese sausage (about 2 ounces), thinly sliced on the diagonal

1 green onion, chopped

1 tsp. chopped cilantro

In a small bowl, soak the mushrooms in warm water to cover until softened, about 20 minutes; drain. Discard the stems and thinly slice the caps.

Preheat the oven to 350 degrees F.

In a 1-quart clay pot, combine the broth, rice, soy sauce, ginger, and mushrooms. Place over medium-high heat and bring to a boil. Lay the duck and sausage on top of the rice. Cover the pot and transfer to the oven. Bake until the liquid is absorbed, about 25 minutes. Garnish with the green onion and cilantro and serve right from the pot.

MAKES 4 SERVINGS

CLAY-POT COOKING

Many ancient cultures cooked in earthenware pots, and Chinese cooks still do. They favor clay pots because they produce succulent braised or stewed dishes that are lower in fat. The food slow-cooks, simmering in its own sealed-in juices, resulting in a sensational dish with mingled flavors. You can serve meals directly in attractive, earth-toned clay pots, often fired into interesting shapes to make elegant serving ware. Remember, never place a hot clay pot on a cold surface or, instead of having a clay pot, you'll have a crackpot!

Grandma Yan's Signature Fried Rice

Yang Chow fried rice is a classic Southern Chinese rice dish. Think of it as the ultimate, deluxe fried rice. I've added a special touch: preserved duck, to go with all the traditional ingredients such as barbecue pork (*char siu*), shrimp, and eggs. This is a perfect one-dish meal.

2 tbsp. vegetable oil

4 cups cold cooked long-grain rice

¼ cup shredded Preserved Duck Legs (page 65)

¼ cup diced Char Siu (page 172)

¼ cup cooked bay shrimp

½ cup shelled or thawed frozen peas

3 tbsp. chopped green onion

2 tsp. salt

⅛ tsp. ground white pepper

3 eggs, beaten

1 tsp. sesame oil

Place a wok or stir-fry pan over high heat until hot. Add the oil, swirling to coat the sides. Add the rice, separating the grains with the back of a spoon. Stir in the duck, *char siu*, and shrimp and cook until the meats are heated through, 2 to 3 minutes. Add the peas, green onion, salt, and white pepper and stir to combine. Make a well in the center of the rice, add the eggs, and gently stir until they form soft curds, about 1 minute. Stir to mix the eggs into the rice. Add the sesame oil and toss to combine.

Transfer to a serving platter and serve.

MAKES 4 SERVINGS

Vegetarian Fried Brown Rice

Cooks in many tribal areas in Western China are putting an interesting spin on their fried rice. They use brown (unmilled) rice, and for a little extra crunch, they add high mountain barley. For this recipe, I took out the barley but kept the brown rice. With all the accompanying vegetables, it's still mighty crunchy.

½ cup shelled green soybeans (edamame), thawed if frozen

2 tbsp. vegetable oil

3 tbsp. minced ginger

5 cups cold cooked brown rice

2 tbsp. Chinese rice wine or dry sherry

1 cup cooked diced carrot, thawed if frozen

1 cup fresh or thawed frozen corn kernels

3 tbsp. soy sauce

¾ tsp. salt

⅛ tsp. ground white pepper

2 eggs, lightly beaten

2 tbsp. sesame oil

1 tbsp. julienned red pickled ginger (optional)

Bring a small saucepan filled with water to a boil over high heat. Add the soybeans and cook until tender-crisp, about 3 minutes; drain and set aside.

Place a wok or stir-fry pan over high heat until hot. Add the vegetable oil, swirling to coat the sides. Add the ginger and cook, stirring until fragrant, about 10 seconds. Add the rice, separating the grains with the back of a spoon. Stir in the rice wine, soybeans, carrot, and corn and cook until the rice is heated through, 2 to 3 minutes. Add the soy sauce, salt, and pepper and stir to combine. Make a well in the center of the rice, add the eggs, and gently stir the eggs until they form soft curds, about 1 minute. Stir to mix the eggs into the rice. Add the sesame oil, and stir to combine.

Transfer to a serving plate and garnish with the pickled ginger, if desired.

MAKES 4 SERVINGS

Pressed Rice Cakes

Street food has always been a big part of Chinese food culture. Even with all the spanking new shopping malls and food courts, on the side streets of every Chinese city are food vendors offering a variety of treats. I found these rice cakes all over China, and people absolutely adore them! They take them on buses and trains—everywhere they go.

2 cups raw glutinous rice

3 cups water

1 tsp. salt

3 tsp. minced garlic

1 tbsp. vegetable oil

½ cup pork *sung*

1 tbsp. finely chopped pickled garlic

1 tbsp. finely chopped Sichuan preserved vegetables

4 fresh banana leaves (optional)

3 tbsp. toasted sesame seeds

In a 2-quart pan, combine the rice, water, salt, and 1 tsp. of the minced garlic. Bring to a boil over high heat, reduce the heat to low, and simmer, covered, until all the liquid is absorbed, about 40 minutes.

Meanwhile, place the oil and remaining 2 tsp. minced garlic in a small saucepan and heat over medium-low heat until the garlic is golden brown. Set aside to cool.

Combine the pork *sung*, pickled garlic, preserved vegetables, and three-quarters of the garlic-oil mixture in a small bowl and mix well. Set aside.

Line a loaf pan with plastic wrap or banana leaves and brush with some of the remaining garlic oil. Sprinkle with half of the toasted sesame seeds. Spoon half of the rice into the lined pan and work with wet hands to press the rice into an even layer. Sprinkle the pork *sung* mixture evenly over the rice and cover with the remaining rice. Sprinkle with the remaining sesame seeds and cover with more oiled plastic or leaves and a second square pan. Weight the top pan down with a few cans.

Let stand for at least 20 minutes. Invert onto a cutting board, remove the plastic or leaves, and slice into 1½-inch squares with a wet knife. Serve at room temperature as is, or lightly pan-fry until crisp.

MAKES 6 RICE CAKES

Red and Gold Fried Rice

This dish combines two Canton classics: tomato beef and fried rice. Tasty and fulfilling, it's also quick and easy to make. The dash of ketchup gives a nice tangy taste to the silky scrambled eggs.

4 dried black mushrooms

2 tbsp. vegetable oil

¼ cup chopped onion

1 tbsp. minced ginger

4 ounces ground beef

3 cups cold cooked long-grain rice

1½ cups cherry tomatoes, halved

¼ cup sliced green onions

2 tbsp. ketchup

1 tbsp. Rich Homemade Broth (page 49) or canned chicken broth

1 tbsp. soy sauce

2 tsp. hoisin sauce

¾ tsp. salt

4 eggs, lightly beaten

In a small bowl, soak the mushrooms in warm water to cover until softened, about 20 minutes; drain. Discard the stems and chop the caps.

Place a wok or stir-fry pan over medium-high heat until hot. Add the oil, swirling to coat the sides. Add the onion and ginger and cook, stirring, until fragrant, about 30 seconds. Add the beef and mushrooms and stir-fry until the meat is no longer pink, about 2 minutes. Add the rice, separating the grains with the back of a spoon, and cook until the rice is heated through. Add the tomatoes, green onions, ketchup, broth, soy sauce, hoisin sauce, and salt and stir to combine. Make a well in the center of the rice, add the eggs, and gently stir the eggs until they form soft curds, about 1 minute. Stir to mix the eggs into the rice.

Transfer to a serving plate and serve.

MAKES 4 SERVINGS

CHINESE SYMBOLS

Not too prosperous this year? Maybe you forgot to eat chicken on New Year's. The Chinese believe in the power of symbols. Chicken is served whole on Chinese New Year, symbolizing family and unity. Colors also play a big role in events like weddings and birthdays. Red and gold represent wealth, good fortune, and vitality; they are the primary colors of Chinese culture. The numbers 3, 8, and 9 promote good luck because they are phonetically similar to words like "fortune" and "prosperity." The number 4, however, sounds like "death," so don't be surprised when the 4th floor of your Chinese hotel is missing.

Crispy Tofu Chow Fun
with Chili Sauce

Tofu may be flavor-neutral, but it's anything but boring. Fried tofu, for instance, comes in different shapes, sizes, and forms, each the perfect partner to a different kind of dish. I sprinkle crispy fried tofu on soft fresh rice noodles (*chow fun*), which provides great texture contrast.

Vegetable oil for deep-frying

8 ounces firm tofu, drained and diced

¼ cup cornstarch

SEASONING

3 tbsp. regular soy sauce

2 tsp. dark soy sauce

½ tsp. sugar

¼ tsp. salt

1 pound fresh rice noodles, about ½ inch wide, noodles separated

SAUCE

½ cup Rich Homemade Broth (page 49) or canned chicken broth

2 tbsp. Chinese rice wine or dry sherry

1 tbsp. vegetarian stir-fry sauce or oyster-flavored sauce

1 tbsp. Chef Yan's Chili Sauce (page 56) or store-bought XO sauce

¼ tsp. salt

1 tsp. minced garlic

1 tsp. minced ginger

½ cup sugar snap peas

¼ cup chopped onion

½ red bell pepper, seeded and cut into narrow strips

1½ tsp. cornstarch dissolved in 1 tbsp. water

Pour oil to a depth of 2 inches into a 2-quart saucepan and heat to 375 degrees F on a deep-fry thermometer. Pat the tofu dry with paper towels. Lightly dust the tofu with the cornstarch. Add the tofu and deep-fry until golden brown and crisp, about 5 minutes. Remove the tofu with a wire strainer or slotted spoon and drain on paper towels. Set aside. Carefully pour the oil into a heatproof bowl, reserving the oil.

To make the seasoning, combine the regular and dark soy sauce and sugar and salt in a small bowl, stirring until the sugar and salt dissolve. Place a wok or stir-fry pan over high heat and add 2 tbsp. of the reserved oil, swirling to coat the sides. Add the noodles and cook, stirring, until they are evenly coated in the oil. Pour in the seasoning and stir-fry until the noodles absorb the liquid, about 1 minute. Transfer the noodles to a warm serving plate. Cover loosely with foil to keep warm.

To make the sauce, combine the broth, wine, stir-fry sauce, chili sauce, and salt in a small bowl. Return the wok or stir-fry pan to high heat. Add 2 tbsp. of the reserved oil, swirling to coat the sides. Discard any remaining oil, or strain and save for another use. Add the garlic and ginger and cook, stirring, until fragrant, about 20 seconds. Add the sugar snap peas and onion and stir-fry until tender-crisp, about 2 minutes. Add the sauce and bring to a boil. Add the tofu and bell pepper, stirring to combine. Add the cornstarch mixture and cook until the sauce boils and thickens.

Pour the sauce and vegetables over the noodles and serve.

MAKES 4 SERVINGS

WOK TO ENLIGHTENMENT

Buddhism, a tradition that spread in China because it echoes the Chinese classic philosophy of life, "the way of Tao," emphasizes doing anything with great thought, whether it's drinking tea or doing calisthenics. It's no surprise to see Buddhist monks practicing martial arts. No, they're not escaping long hours of boring meditation. . . they're actually practicing a form of meditation in action. My way of meditating is behind a wok.

A Nation in Celebration

In China, no celebration compares with the Chinese New Year. Instead of one night of merriment and debauchery, culminating in a midnight countdown, we party for weeks! As we herald a New Year, we pay close attention to the symbolism around us. Cherry blossoms represent new bloom and good fortune. Kumquats (*kum-quat* = gold-lucky) and mandarin oranges (*da-ji* = big luck) promise prosperity. It's a good idea to eat apples (*ping-guo* = a smooth result) or pomelos (*luk-yao* = something's continually coming). In the north, families gather to cook dumplings in boiling water, suggesting excitement. In the south, deep-fried dumplings pop open in hot oil, just as life should pop open with surprises.

During the Lantern Festival, the fifteenth day of the New Year, people gather to admire colorful lanterns in the streets and on the waters. The cold north "lights the way for the future" with beautiful ice-carved lanterns. Throughout the country, people eat sesame seed rice balls because roundness symbolizes harmony, and sweet sticky-rice pancakes called *nan-gao* (climbing higher–getting better), which sums up hopes for the coming year.

China's most ancient holiday, Double Fifth Day (the fifth day of the fifth month), is also known as the Dragon Boat Festival. Originally a ritual to ward off disease, it evolved into a tribute to minister/poet Chu Yuan (circa 300 B.C.), a legendary figure who fought corruption and committed ritual suicide by jumping into the Miluo River. His loyal constituents rushed out in dragon boats to recover the body, throwing rice tamales into the water in hopes that the fish would find them tastier than Chu Yuan. Today, both disease-defying symbols and dragon boat races commemorate the day, and everyone enjoys *zongzi*, cone-shaped tamales wrapped in bamboo or lotus leaves. Sweet fillings consist of mung beans, dates, and bean paste; savory ones contain *char siu* (barbecued pork), Chinese sausage, mushrooms, duck eggs, chestnuts, peanuts, or dried shrimp.

Zhong-qiu means "middle autumn" and also "get together," so it's a perfect time to get together for a harvest celebration! Historians credit the Autumn Festival's moon cake for changing Chinese history. The patriot Shu Yuan Zhang devised a scheme for overthrowing the Yuan Dynasty and tucked detailed copies of his attack plan into moon-shaped cakes. He convinced Yuan officials that the cakes were festive gifts and distributed them to fellow revolutionaries. The coup succeeded and China's Ming Empire was established. Today, these sweet bean or lotus seed cakes are common gifts. But instead of revolutionary messages, expect to find duck eggs and other sumptuous fillings inside.

All around China, you can find regional festivals. Recently, I joined the Musuo Tribe in southwestern China for their Round Mountain Festival. People trek or ride on horseback through mountains to attend this annual tribute to the heavens, mountains, and water. It's a chance for distant friends and relatives to reconnect. We prayed together, burned incense, hung prayer flags, and threw rice skyward to ensure abundant crops, then feasted on preserved pork, roasted goat, and grilled vegetables. Famous for their a cappella singing, the Musuo rounded out the evening with songs of praise to nature.

It must be radar—somehow, it seems no matter where or when I travel in China, I bump into a major festival with unusual customs and really fantastic food!

Double Happiness Pasta

In Shanxi, noodles are handmade, often right in front of diners. Noodle chefs work up to ten hours a day, serving hundreds of noodle fans. Kneading dough for ten straight hours wouldn't do much to double my happiness! I'm glad I'm not a noodle chef.

NOODLE BASKET

6 ounces fresh Chinese egg noodles

Vegetable oil for deep-frying

1½ cups small dry pasta, such as small shells or elbow macaroni

4 tsp. Chinese black vinegar or balsamic vinegar

2 tsp. sesame oil

SAUCE

⅓ cup chopped onion

⅓ cup diced red bell pepper

2 tsp. minced garlic

4 ounces ground meat

¾ cup Rich Homemade Broth (page 49) or canned chicken broth

¼ cup Chinese black vinegar or balsamic vinegar

¼ cup chili garlic sauce

2 tbsp. soy sauce

1 tbsp. sugar

¼ tsp. Sichuan peppercorns, toasted and ground

1 tsp. cornstarch dissolved in 2 tsp. water

2 green onions, thinly sliced

To make the noodle basket, bring a large pot of water to a boil over high heat. Add the fresh noodles and cook according to package directions. Drain, rinse with cold water, and drain again. Pour vegetable oil to a depth of 3 inches into a wok or stir-fry pan. Heat to 360 degrees F on a deep-fry thermometer. Line the bottom of a large wire strainer (at least 8 inches in diameter) with the noodles. Put another wire strainer on top of the noodles to keep them secure. Gently lower the noodles, held between the 2 strainers, into the hot oil. Deep-fry until golden and crisp, about 5 minutes. Set aside to drain on paper towels. Carefully pour the oil into a heatproof bowl, reserving the oil.

Bring another large pot of water to a boil over high heat. Add the small dry pasta and cook according to the package directions. Drain. Transfer to a large bowl. Add the vinegar and sesame oil. Toss to coat evenly. Set aside.

To make the sauce, place a clean wok or stir-fry pan over medium-high heat. Add 3 tbsp. of the reserved vegetable oil, swirling to coat the sides. Discard any remaining oil, or strain and save for another use. Add the onion, bell pepper, and garlic and cook, stirring, until fragrant, about 30 seconds. Add the meat and continue to cook until it is no longer pink, about 3 minutes. Add the broth, vinegar, chili garlic sauce, soy sauce, sugar, and peppercorns and bring to a boil. Add the cornstarch mixture and cook, stirring, until the sauce boils and thickens, about 30 seconds. Add the pasta and stir to coat in the sauce until heated through.

Transfer the noodle basket to a serving plate. Pour the pasta and the sauce into the noodle basket, garnish with the green onions, and serve.

MAKES 6 SERVINGS

Pan-Fried Noodle Cakes

These are called noodle cakes because they are flat and resemble pancakes in a wok. In Guangzhou and Hong Kong, they are called *liang mein huang*, which means "crispy on both sides." This is a classic Cantonese dish that goes well with a wide variety of proteins and vegetables.

16 ounces fresh Chinese
egg noodles

5 tbsp. vegetable oil

½ cup Rich Homemade
Broth (page 49) or canned
chicken broth

Preheat the oven to 200 degrees F. Bring a large pot filled with water to a boil over high heat. Add the noodles and cook according to the package directions. Drain, rinse with cold water, and drain again. Return the noodles to the pot (off the heat) and toss with 1 tbsp. of the oil.

Place a wide, nonstick frying pan over medium heat until hot. Add 2 tbsp. of the oil, swirling to coat the bottom. Spread half of the noodles (about 2 cups) evenly in the pan. Add half of the broth and cook until the liquid is evaporated and the noodles are golden brown, about 5 minutes. Flip the pancake and cook on the second side until golden brown, about 5 minutes. Transfer the noodle pancake to a large, heatproof serving platter and keep warm in the oven. Cook the remaining noodles in the same way, using the remaining 2 tbsp. oil and ¼ cup broth.

Serve topped with a stir-fry dish.

MAKES 2 NOODLE CAKES

LONG LIVE NOODLES!

Nearly every culture boasts great noodle dishes. But where did noodles originate? At last, China can proudly assert itself as the birthplace of all noodles. Recently, archaeologists discovered the remains of the world's oldest noodles, in Lajia, along the Yellow River. The 50-centimeter-long, yellow, hand-pulled strands, buried in an earthenware bowl, carbon-date back four thousand years. So there you have it: the world's oldest leftovers!

When it comes to Chinese noodles, length truly does matter. Want to assure a long life, blissful marriage, or lucrative business venture? Celebrate your birthday, wedding, or grand opening by slurping down long noodles! In fact, noodles make great symbolic gifts for any occasion marking a long relationship.

With four thousand years of practice, it's no wonder that Chinese cooks know a thing or two about cooking noodles. Of the primary types of noodles, wheat flour noodles, or *mein*, made with or without eggs, originated in the north, where wheat is commonly cultivated. Rice noodles, or *fun*, consisting of rice flour with water, come from China's many rice-growing regions in the south. Clear noodles, *fun sze* or *fan pei*, are created from ground mung bean paste. Chinese noodles are served cold, steamed, stir-fried, deep-fried, and boiled. They are tossed with sauce as a main course or used in soups, salads, and even desserts.

You might find noodles in a variety of colors at your Chinese market—yellow from eggs, green with ground tea or spinach, or tinged purple by taro root, for example. Although most noodles are processed by machine, "hand-pulling" noodles remains a classic culinary art still practiced by Chinese noodle chefs. In Shanxi Province—the noodle capital of China— you can find chefs hand-pulling noodles in many popular noodle restaurants. It takes years of practice to perfect the technique of stretching and twirling the dough until it's the right length and elasticity. After repeated folding, the prepared dough can then be cut into noodles that are broad and fat or thin like string, but never, never cut short!

Dry-Fried Glass Noodles

Made of mung bean flour, bean thread noodles are also called glass noodles or cellophane noodles because they are transparent when cooked. By themselves, the noodles are not particularly flavorful. However, they can take on all the flavors of accompanying ingredients and spices. Leave out the meat in this recipe and you can serve it as a vegetarian dish.

4 ounces dried bean
thread noodles

MARINADE

1 tbsp. rice vinegar

2 tsp. soy sauce

2 tsp. cornstarch

4 ounces ground meat

3 tbsp. vegetable oil

1 tsp. minced garlic

½ tsp. minced ginger

1 tbsp. chili bean paste

3 whole dried red chiles

1 tsp. soy sauce

½ tsp. salt

1 green onion, chopped

¼ tsp. sesame oil

½ fresh hot chile, sliced
into rings, for garnish

Pour enough warm water over the noodles in a large bowl to cover completely. Soak until softened, about 10 minutes. Drain thoroughly. Cut the noodles with scissors into 3-inch-long pieces.

To make the marinade, combine the rice vinegar, soy sauce, and cornstarch in a bowl and mix well. Add the meat and stir to coat evenly. Let stand for 10 minutes.

Place a wok or stir-fry pan over high heat until hot. Add the oil, swirling to coat the sides. Add the garlic, ginger, bean paste, and dried chiles and cook, stirring, until fragrant. Add the meat and stir-fry until it is no longer pink, about 2 minutes. Add the soy sauce, salt, and noodles and cook, stirring, until well mixed, about 4 minutes. Stir in the green onion and sesame oil.

Transfer to a serving plate, garnish with the fresh chile, and serve.

MAKES 6 SERVINGS

Noodle Salad with Peanut Dressing

These days, chilled noodles are lauded as a new discovery in the West. Of course, in Sichuan, noodles have been served chilled as long as noodles have been served. There is a notable difference in this recipe, however. Instead of the traditional sesame seed paste dressing, this recipe uses a peanut dressing.

8 ounces fresh Chinese egg noodles	½ red bell pepper, seeded and julienned	1 tsp. Chili Oil (page 58) or a store-bought version
2 cups bean sprouts	1 tsp. salt	1 cup Peanut Dressing (page 57)
3 green onions, julienned	⅛ tsp. ground white pepper	¼ cup chopped roasted peanuts
½ cup cilantro leaves		

Bring a large pot filled with water to a boil over high heat. Add the noodles and cook according to the package directions. Drain, rinse with cold water, and drain again.

Place the noodles in a large bowl with the bean sprouts, green onions, half of the cilantro leaves, the bell pepper, salt, white pepper, and chili oil. Pour the dressing over the noodles and toss to coat evenly.

Sprinkle the peanuts and remaining cilantro leaves over the top. Transfer to a serving plate and serve chilled or at room temperature.

MAKES 4 SERVINGS

Entrées

Picture a group of professional chefs around the dinner table. What are they talking about? Politics? Sports? Religion? The weather? No! They are talking about food. Professional chefs are people of great passion. And a gathering of like-minded professionals is the perfect forum to let loose their zeal. What greater joy in life is there than to share your knowledge and opinions with those who are truly your peers? In my many visits to China, I've treasured all the special dinners I've shared with my fellow chefs. Those were evenings of true enlightenment, and the great food that followed was simply an added bonus.

At a recent hot-pot gathering, I was comparing notes with other chefs on the different genres of hot chiles they use in the popular yin-yang hot pot (for my version, see Sichuan Hot Pot, page 187). The consensus around the table was that round red chiles top the scale. They certainly do for me. After each taste, I had to down a glass of water before taking the next bite. In fact, to this day, every time I think of that evening, my eyes water and my nose itches.

Traveling to Shangri-la was a real adventure. The scenery was absolutely stunning: snowcapped mountains, even in July, with narrow mountain paths leading down to lush green valleys. It was an earthly paradise. Equally fascinating was the exotic cuisine. I am well acquainted with mutton, but yak? It was a taste I acquired in no time.

On another memorable evening in Beijing, I found myself arguing about the origins of what North Americans call sweet-and-sour (Beijing Sweet-and-Sour Spareribs, page 170). I know that sweet-and-sour is a must-have on the menu of every Chinese-American restaurant. And seeing that most early Chinese immigrants in North America originated in Canton, I had automatically linked sweet-and-sour to Southern China. "Not so!" proclaimed my Northern Chinese colleagues. According to them, sweet-and-sour originated in Beijing, and the true taste profile is more tangy (sour) than sweet, on account of the black vinegar that's common in Northern cuisine. What can I say? Some like it sweet, some like it sour. Me, I like it for dinner.

Lacquered Black Bean Salmon

Salmon is a relatively new favorite among the Chinese. It's gaining popularity in major cities such as Shanghai and Hong Kong, which are awash in international restaurants. This East-meets-West recipe combines the traditional Chinese flavor of salted black beans with salmon.

MARINADE

¼ cup light soy sauce

¼ cup dark soy sauce

½ cup honey

1 pound center-cut salmon fillet, cut into 4 equal pieces

8 ounces Chinese long beans

2 tbsp. Black Bean Sauce (page 41) or a store-bought version

3 tbsp. rice vinegar

2 tsp. cornstarch dissolved in 4 tsp. water

Preheat the oven to 450 degrees F. Line a small baking pan with a large piece of aluminum foil, allowing the excess to hang over the sides.

To make the marinade, combine the light and dark soy sauces and honey in a wide, medium bowl and mix well. Add the salmon and stir to coat evenly. Let stand for 10 minutes.

Bring a large pot of water to a boil. Add the long beans and blanch until tender-crisp, 2 to 3 minutes. Drain. Transfer to a serving platter. Set aside.

Transfer the salmon to a cutting board, skin side down, reserving the marinade. Score each piece of the salmon, through the flesh side, ½ inch deep, creating a little pocket. Fill each pocket with some of the black bean sauce. Put the salmon pieces in the center of the foil. Lift the sides of the foil up and over the salmon to create a sealed packet. Bake until just cooked through, 5 to 8 minutes. While the salmon is baking, combine the reserved marinade and rice vinegar together in a small saucepan and bring to a boil. Add the cornstarch mixture and stir until the sauce thickens.

Transfer the salmon to the platter with the long beans. Pour the sauce over all and serve.

MAKES 4 SERVINGS

Black Vinegar–Flavored Fish

Popular in Northern China, black vinegar has a smoky, sweet flavor and is made by fermenting rice, wheat, millet, or sorghum. It is more full-bodied and well-rounded than regular distilled vinegar. The addition of pickled garlic cloves adds flavor and texture to this tangy dish. They are widely available in Asian markets and often come in sealed glass jars from China or Thailand.

¼ cup dried wood ear mushrooms

MARINADE

1 tsp. vegetable oil

1 tbsp. cornstarch

½ tsp. salt

⅛ tsp. ground white pepper

1 pound white fish fillets, such as cod, halibut, or rockfish, cut into 4 equal pieces

SAUCE

1½ cups Rich Homemade Broth (page 49) or canned chicken broth

½ cup Chinese black vinegar or balsamic vinegar

2 tbsp. hoisin sauce

2 tbsp. Chinese rice wine or dry sherry

1 tbsp. soy sauce

1 tbsp. sugar

2 tbsp. vegetable oil

1 tbsp. Chinese rice wine or dry sherry

20 cloves pickled garlic

3 tbsp. shredded ginger

4 green onions, chopped

1 tsp. Chili Oil (page 58) or store-bought chili oil

⅛ tsp. ground white pepper

1 tbsp. red pickled ginger, shredded (optional)

In a bowl, soak the mushrooms in warm water to cover until softened, about 30 minutes; drain. Thinly slice the mushrooms and set aside.

To make the marinade, combine the oil, cornstarch, salt, and white pepper in a medium, shallow bowl and mix well. Add the fish and stir to coat evenly. Set aside.

To make the sauce, combine the broth, black vinegar, hoisin sauce, rice wine, soy sauce, and sugar in a medium bowl. Add the sliced mushrooms and mix well.

Place a wok or stir-fry pan over high heat until hot. Add the oil, swirling to coat the sides. Add the fish and fry until golden, about 1 minute per side. Add the rice wine and cook until evaporated, about 30 seconds. Add the pickled garlic, shredded ginger, and green onions and stir-fry, about 1 minute. Add the sauce and bring to a boil. Reduce the heat to medium-low, cover, and simmer until the fish turns opaque, about 5 minutes. Add the chili oil and white pepper and stir to combine.

Transfer to a serving plate, garnish with the pickled ginger (if using), and serve.

MAKES 4 SERVINGS

VENI, VIDI, VINEGAR!

Shanxi Province produces a rich, tangy black vinegar comparable to the most expensive balsamic vinegar from Italy. My visit to the Aged Vinegar Factory was a culinary journey for the senses. Tears welled in my eyes, not from the excitement of finding such an exquisite condiment, but because of the overwhelming fumes of the fermented, aged vinegar. This 2,500-year-old factory ages its vinegar in a special sunroom from 1 to 10 years. The rich, tangy, and sweet taste will entertain all your taste buds.

Room for Another Course?

Life is a banquet, as anyone in China will tell you. Every businessperson who's visited China can attest to attending numerous multicourse banquets. Even tourists are not immune. As you read this, some helpless tour group in China is being overindulged with an extravagant eight-course banquet meal: lion head meatballs, shallow-fried tiger prawns, whole grouper steamed and drizzled with spicy hot oil . . . those Chinese tour operators can be merciless!

What to do when confronted with such a dilemma? Here's Martin Yan's guide to surviving a Chinese banquet: First of all, know that a formal Chinese banquet is culinary theater. Everyone—and that includes you, the guest—has a role to play. At the reception area, the host greets each guest with exaggerated enthusiasm and, even at a lavish feast, apologizes for the meager offerings about to be shared. The main guest is seated in the lucky right side of the room, while the humble host takes the least honorable seat.

Banquets begin when the host toasts *gan bei* (empty glass). Glasses filled before each course symbolize full respect for each guest and must be drained to demonstrate complete gratefulness. Traditionally, food is first offered to ancestors. No one eats until the honored guest is served or the host gives the "raise the chopsticks" sign. Exquisite food is the banquet's focus, and the host's concern is to continually excite the guests' palates.

Instead of soup, delicate dishes with subtle flavors come first. Then come richer entrées with stronger sauces, followed by soup and robust dishes. Fish, *yu* (abundance), is served at the end, a symbolic wish that abundant food will always grace your table.

My advice: Take it slow at any Chinese banquet. Just as your tummy begins groaning and you think, "I'll never, ever be hungry again!" you won't believe what's coming next!

Chinese New Year banquets, always a "good" number of eight or nine courses, include a whole fish, chicken, and duck. The complete menu consists of symbolic foods, all to ensure a new year of luck and fortune. Chinese wedding banquets differ by region, but all include two things: a whole chicken and noodles. Longevity banquets are birthday parties for elderly people. Even people's passing is honored with a banquet that can last up to forty-nine days! The more you banquet, the more you honor the departed.

Some banquets are held in honor of local foods. At Beijing's Peking duck banquets, every dish includes a part of the duck. Southern China specializes in seafood banquets. Shanxi people celebrate with a drunken banquet, incorporating wine in all dishes. Yunnan holds plum banquets, mushroom banquets, and spring banquets, with dishes infused with all types of flowers. Beijing's imperial banquet, from the majestic greeting to the royal escort out, reenacts emperors' feasts. Though you'll be an emperor or empress for only a day, you'll taste an extraordinary banquet with up to 108 dishes, each a work of art.

Up in the mountain enclaves of Western China, the natives banquet just as passionately as the rest of the country. I attended a thirty-nine-course banquet— three "waves" of thirteen dishes each—hosted by Chef Jun in his native Naxi village. Imagine: Our first course was sweets! The second course was composed of refined delicacies showcasing my host's artistry, and the grand finale third was made up of Naxi home-style dishes, including the famous Yunnan-style hot pot. What a sumptuous meal!

So wherever you plan to go in China, don't forget to pack your appetite—and clothing with an expandable waistband.

Spice Market Fish

Not all spicy dishes are from Sichuan, and not all Sichuan dishes are spicy. However, Sichuan dishes do tend to have a rich profusion of flavors—a result of carefully mixed spices. This recipe reflects this culinary practice. I like the addition of cilantro; it highlights the fresh spices. For a different taste sensation, add mint.

SAUCE

1½ cups bottled clam juice

¼ cup ketchup

2 tbsp. chili bean paste

2 tbsp. rice vinegar

1 tbsp. vegetable oil

5 cloves garlic, peeled and halved

1 tsp. minced ginger

12 ounces white fish fillet, such as halibut, snapper, or grouper, cut into 1-inch pieces

2 green onions, chopped

1 tsp. sesame oil

1 fresh hot red chile, thinly sliced

8 cherry tomatoes

4 sprigs cilantro, for garnish

To make the sauce, combine the clam juice, ketchup, chili bean paste, and rice vinegar in a medium bowl and mix well.

Place a wok or stir-fry pan over medium-high heat until hot. Add the oil, swirling to coat the sides. Add the garlic and ginger and cook, stirring, until fragrant, about 20 seconds. Add the sauce and bring to a boil. Add the fish and half of the green onions and return to a boil. Reduce the heat to medium-low, cover, and simmer until the fish is cooked through, about 5 minutes. Add the sesame oil, chile, and tomatoes and cook for 5 minutes more.

Transfer to a serving bowl. Garnish with the cilantro and remaining green onions and serve.

MAKES 4 SERVINGS

A TRIP DOWN SENSORY LANE

Sichuan, the Chinese gate to the historic Silk Road, is the Mecca of spice. If you're walking briskly through the spice market, you're probably looking for a glass of water to douse the heat of the Sichuan peppercorns you just sampled. You pass though mountains of red chiles, peppercorns, and star anise, inhaling the intoxicating scent of cinnamon, clove, and sweet fennel seed. It's really using your senses!

Prosperity Steamed Fish

In China, fish is a symbol of wealth and prosperity. Steamed fish is a popular dish to serve during special occasions, such as formal banquets and holiday dinners. It is a permanent fixture on any Chinese New Year menu. When serving fish on such an occasion, serve it whole—head, tail, and all. This symbolizes a good beginning and a good ending.

One 1½- to 2-pound whole fish, such as rockfish or snapper, cleaned

¼ tsp. salt

⅛ tsp. ground white pepper

3 tbsp. soy sauce

1 tsp. sesame oil

4 sprigs cilantro

3 tbsp. vegetable oil

Prepare a wok or stir-fry pan for steaming (see page 23). Season the fish inside and out with the salt and pepper. Place the fish on an 8- or 9-inch pie plate or shallow, heatproof dish. Place the dish in the steamer, cover, and steam over high heat until the fish turns opaque and just begins to flake, 15 to 20 minutes. Carefully remove the dish from the steamer.

Stir the soy sauce and sesame oil together in a small bowl. Pour over the steamed fish. Lay the cilantro sprigs over the top of the fish.

In a small skillet, heat the vegetable oil over high heat until it just begins to smoke. Carefully pour the hot oil over the fish, stand back, and watch it sizzle. Serve immediately.

MAKES 4 SERVINGS

DON'T JUST CHANGE YOUR OIL, COOK IT!

A good Chinese chef can differentiate cooked oil from uncooked oil, much the same way that anyone can tell inexpensive from extra-virgin olive oil. Many Chinese prefer the taste of seasoned oils, so they heat it up and add garlic, onion, ginger, and/or chiles. The flavors infuse the oil and add great taste to stir-fried food. Also, by heating oil before pouring it over steamed fish, the fishy odor is eliminated, and the oil creates a pleasant sizzle.

Steamed Fish Fillet in Black Bean Sauce

Cantonese chefs love steaming whole fish. However, in the West, where many meals are prepared for just one or two people, steaming fish fillets is often more practical. Instead of having to clean and prepare a whole fish for the meal, purchase your favorite fish fillet from the store.

1 ounce dried bean thread noodles

1 tbsp. vegetable oil

½ tsp. minced garlic

½ tsp. minced ginger

4 tsp. salted black beans, rinsed and lightly mashed

2 tbsp. Rich Homemade Broth (page 49) or canned chicken broth

1 tbsp. Chinese rice wine or dry sherry

1 tbsp. chili garlic sauce

⅛ tsp. ground white pepper

1 pound white fish fillet, such as halibut or cod

8 cherry tomatoes

½ tsp. sesame oil

3 sprigs cilantro

In a medium bowl, soak the bean thread noodles in warm water to cover until softened, about 15 minutes. Drain and set aside.

Place a wok or stir-fry pan over high heat until hot. Add the oil, swirling to coat the sides. Add the garlic, ginger, and black beans and cook, stirring, until fragrant, about 15 seconds. Add the broth, rice wine, chili garlic sauce, and white pepper and cook until the sauce thickens slightly, about 2 minutes. Transfer to a large bowl and set aside to cool.

Cut the fish into 4 equal pieces. Transfer it to the cooled black bean mixture and stir to coat. Let stand for 15 minutes.

Prepare a wok or stir-fry pan for steaming (see page 23). Place the softened bean thread noodles in a shallow, heatproof dish. Arrange the fish and black bean sauce and tomatoes over the noodles. Place the dish in the steamer, cover, and steam over high heat until the fish turns opaque and just begins to flake, about 10 minutes.

Drizzle the sesame oil over the fish, garnish with the cilantro, and serve.

MAKES 4 SERVINGS

CATCH OF THE DAY

The Cantonese word for seafood is *hoisin*, which literally means "fresh from the sea." In large Chinese seafood restaurants you will find dozens of fresh and salt water tanks. You can dive into your choice of lobsters, shrimp, crabs, sea bass, catfish, turtles, and even eels.

Imperial Sweet-and-Sour Fish

....

This is a spectacular banquet dish that's also ideal for a dinner party at home. The traditional method of scoring fish before frying helps it cook faster and more evenly. It also allows the seasoning to penetrate the fish and gives it a dramatic presentation at the dinner table.

One 1½- to 2-pound whole fish, such as rockfish or snapper, cleaned

1 tsp. salt

¼ tsp. ground white pepper

2 eggs

2 cups all-purpose flour

Vegetable oil for deep-frying

1½ cups Sweet-and-Sour Sauce (page 48) or a store-bought version

1 mango, peeled, pitted, and cut into small cubes

½ cup chopped pineapple

½ tsp. cornstarch dissolved in 1 tsp. water

1 tsp. chopped cilantro

1 tbsp. chopped red bell pepper

1 tbsp. chopped yellow bell pepper

....

Cut 4 diagonal slashes about ¾ inch deep into both sides of the fish. Rub the salt and white pepper into the slashes. Beat the eggs in a wide bowl, and place the flour in a separate wide bowl. Dip the fish into the egg, drain briefly, then dredge it in the flour, gently shaking off the excess.

In a wok, stir-fry pan, or large, deep skillet, pour oil to a depth of 3 inches and heat to 350 degrees F on a deep-fry thermometer. Carefully lower the fish into the hot oil. Use a ladle to carefully and continuously pour hot oil over the top of the fish. Deep-fry until the fish is cooked through, 12 to 15 minutes. Using 2 wire strainers, carefully lift the fish from the hot oil and drain on paper towels.

Bring the sweet-and-sour sauce to a boil in a saucepan. Add the mango and pineapple and cook until the fruit is just heated through, about 1 minute. Add the cornstarch mixture and cook, stirring, until the sauce boils and thickens, about 30 seconds.

Transfer the fish to a serving plate. Pour the sauce over the fish, garnish with the cilantro and red and yellow bell peppers, and serve.

MAKES 4 SERVINGS

Seafood Cloud

....

Fresh seafood tends to send me to cloud nine, so this dish is aptly named. Light and fluffy, egg whites accent the seafood, and don't rain on its parade. This classic dish is served in many Cantonese seafood restaurants.

MARINADE

2 tbsp. Chinese rice wine or dry sherry

½ tsp. salt

⅛ tsp. ground white pepper

4 ounces small raw shrimp, peeled and deveined

4 ounces small scallops

4 ounces skinless salmon fillet, cut into ¾-inch cubes

3 tbsp. vegetable oil

4 whole water chestnuts, coarsely chopped

2 tbsp. fresh or thawed frozen peas

2 egg whites, lightly beaten

1 tsp. fish roe

....

To make the marinade, combine the rice wine, salt, and pepper in a medium bowl and mix well. Add the shrimp, scallops, and salmon and stir to coat evenly. Let stand for 10 minutes.

Place a wok or stir-fry pan over medium-high heat until hot. Add 2 tablespoons of the oil, swirling to coat the sides. Add the seafood and stir-fry until the shrimp turn pink and the scallops and salmon turn opaque, about 2 minutes. Transfer the seafood to a plate and set aside.

Return the wok to medium-high heat. Add the remaining tablespoon of oil, swirling to coat the sides. Add the water chestnuts and peas and cook, stirring, until heated through, about 30 seconds. Pour in the egg whites and cook, stirring, until softly scrambled. Return the seafood to the wok and gently stir until the seafood and egg whites are just combined.

Transfer to a serving plate and garnish with the fish roe. Serve hot.

MAKES 4 SERVINGS

Seafood Trio in a Treasure Chest

With fresh seafood like succulent scallops, fish, and shrimp, this dish might fall victim to marauding dinner guests as they wander through the kitchen. Hide it until you are ready to serve your treasures from the sea. If you like, add a bed of bean thread noodles underneath the Chinese okra to capture all the savory juices.

MARINADE

2 tbsp. fish sauce

2 tsp. soy sauce

2 tsp. sesame oil

2 tsp. minced garlic

1 tsp. Chinese rice wine or dry sherry

⅛ tsp. ground white pepper

8 medium raw shrimp, peeled and deveined

4 sea scallops

4 ounces firm white fish fillet, such as halibut or cod, cut into 4 equal pieces

1 tbsp. vegetable oil

1 pound Chinese okra or zucchini, cut into ¼-inch-thick rounds

2 green onions, green parts only, thinly sliced

¼ red bell pepper, seeded and cut into long, thin strips

Preheat the oven to 400 degrees F.

To make the marinade, combine the fish sauce, soy sauce, sesame oil, garlic, rice wine, and white pepper in a medium bowl. Add the shrimp, scallops, and fish and stir to coat evenly. Let stand for 10 minutes.

Cut four 12-by-18-inch rectangles of parchment paper or heavy-duty foil. Lay them out on a work surface. Lightly brush the center of each square with some of the oil. Divide the okra slices among the pieces of parchment, arranging them in a single layer in the center of each square. Put 2 shrimp, 1 scallop, and 1 piece of fish on top of each okra bed. Spoon some of the marinade over each. Bring the long sides of each parchment rectangle together over the seafood and roll them as one to hold them together. Seal the ends of each packet with a series of small folds. Place the packets on a baking sheet large enough to hold them comfortably. You may need 2 baking sheets.

Bake the seafood packets until the fish is cooked through, 8 to 10 minutes. Transfer each packet to a warm dinner plate. Using the tip of a small, sharp knife, cut a slit in the top of each packet, being careful of the fragrant steam. Open the packets and garnish each with some of the green onions and bell pepper. Serve hot.

MAKES 4 SERVINGS

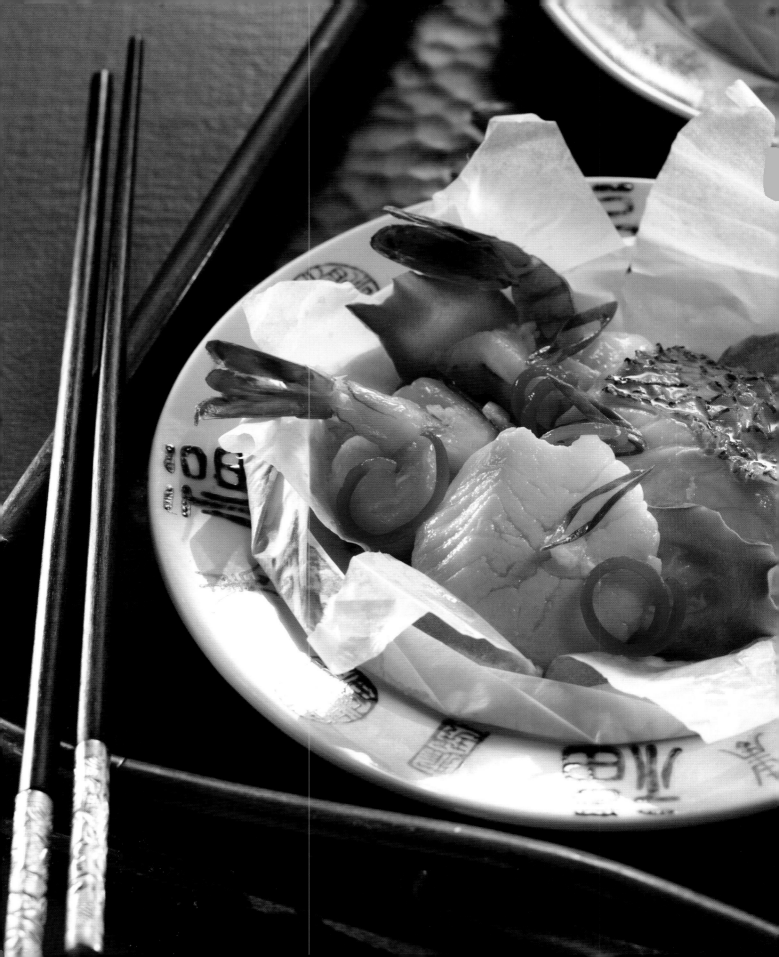

Spicy Garlic Shrimp

I like to cook shrimp in their shells. This keeps them fresh and juicy, plus the shells make a separate treat for us shrimp suckers. If you aren't a "lay out the newspaper on the picnic table" kind of person and finger-lickin' shrimp is not your style, feel free to use peeled shrimp.

1½ pounds large raw, head-on prawns in the shell

MARINADE

1 tbsp. cornstarch

½ tsp. salt

¼ tsp. ground white pepper

SAUCE

¼ cup ketchup

¼ cup Chinese rice wine or dry sherry

¼ cup Rich Homemade Broth (page 49) or canned chicken broth

2 tbsp. chili garlic sauce

2 tsp. honey

1 tsp. sesame oil

1 tsp. soy sauce

2 tbsp. vegetable oil

2 tbsp. minced garlic

1 green onion, chopped

Clip the legs off the prawns with kitchen shears. Rinse the prawns and pat dry with paper towels.

To make the marinade, combine the cornstarch, salt, and white pepper in a large bowl and mix well. Add the prawns and stir gently to coat evenly. Let stand for 10 minutes.

To make the sauce, combine the ketchup, rice wine, broth, chili garlic sauce, honey, sesame oil, and soy sauce in a medium bowl and mix well.

Place a wok or stir-fry pan over high heat until hot. Add 1 tbsp. of the vegetable oil, swirling to coat the sides. Add the garlic and cook, stirring, until fragrant, about 10 seconds. Add the prawns and cook, stirring, until they turn pink, about 1 minute. Transfer the prawns and garlic to a plate and set aside.

Add the remaining 1 tbsp. oil to the pan, swirling to coat the sides. Add the sauce mixture to the pan and cook, stirring occasionally, until the sauce thickens and reduces by half, about 5 minutes. Add the prawn and garlic mixture; toss until the prawns are coated in the sauce and completely cooked through, about 2 minutes.

Transfer to a serving plate, sprinkle with the green onion, and serve.

MAKES 4 SERVINGS

Chef's Fish Basket

Here's an interesting culinary twist: So often we serve fish on a bed of vegetables. This dish does the reverse. The veggies are served inside "baskets" made from boned fish. Such a unique presentation makes it a perfect dish for special banquets and home parties.

4 small whole flatfish (about 4 ounces each), such as pompano, or 1 flounder (about 1 pound)

Vegetable oil for deep-frying

2 ribs celery, finely chopped

½ yellow bell pepper, seeded and chopped

½ red bell pepper, seeded and chopped

2 tsp. fish sauce or oyster-flavored sauce

1 tsp. sesame oil

¾ tsp. salt

¼ tsp. ground white pepper

4 leaves napa cabbage, shredded, for garnish

Using a sharp knife, fillet each fish, reserving the fish frame. Cut the fillets into small cubes and set aside.

Pour the oil into a wok or stir-fry pan to a depth of 2 inches and heat it to 350 degrees F on a deep-fry thermometer. Working with one fish frame at a time, place the frame in a small wire strainer and carefully dip it into the hot oil. Using a ladle, carefully pour the hot oil over the fish frame, gently pressing the frame against the curved bottom of the wire strainer to make a bowl shape. Deep-fry, ladling the hot oil over the fish frame occasionally, until golden and crisp, about 4 minutes. Drain on paper towels. Repeat the process with the remaining fish frames. Carefully pour the oil out into a heatproof bowl. Reserve the oil.

Return the wok to high heat. Add 2 tablespoons of the reserved oil, swirling to coat the sides. Add the celery and bell peppers and cook, stirring, until tender-crisp, about 1 minute. Add the cubed fish and toss for 30 seconds. Add the fish sauce and stir-fry until the fish appears opaque, about 2 minutes. Add the sesame oil, salt, and white pepper and toss until well mixed. Discard any remaining oil, or strain and save for another use.

Make a bed of napa cabbage on a serving platter. Arrange the fish frames, curved side down, on top of the cabbage. Mound the vegetable mixture into each fish "bowl" and serve.

MAKES 4 SERVINGS

CURRY: THE NEW SPICE
ON THE BLOCK

When traders traveling along the Silk
Road brought along Indian spices, the Chinese
picked up curry in a hurry. Currently,
curry is enjoying a wave of popularity
in Cantonese cooking. Uninhibited by the usual
rules that accompany traditional Chinese
ingredients, restaurant chefs and street
vendors curry the favor of
patrons with inventive recipes.

Curry Crab

When it comes to spicy crab, few can surpass Singapore's national dish of chili crab. I was pleasantly surprised when I came upon this Cantonese curry rendition. Live crabs should be refrigerated and are best used within 24 hours. Most fish and crab sellers can clean the crabs for you, saving you prep time and messy counter cleanup.

SAUCE

¾ cup Rich Homemade Broth (page 49) or canned chicken broth

3 tbsp. soy sauce

1 tbsp. curry powder

2 tsp. sugar

¼ tsp. Chinese five-spice powder

1 whole live or cooked Dungeness crab

¼ cup cornstarch

2 tbsp. vegetable oil

½ onion, chopped

2 tbsp. minced garlic

2 tbsp. minced ginger

½ cup unsweetened coconut milk

1 tsp. sesame oil

3 tbsp. diced red bell pepper

1 green onion, chopped

To make the sauce, combine the broth, soy sauce, curry powder, sugar, and five-spice powder in a small bowl and mix well. Set aside.

If cooking a live crab, bring a large pot of water to a boil. Slip the crab into the water and cook for 2 minutes. Drain the crab, rinse under cold water, and drain again. If you like, pull off the top shell in one piece and reserve for garnish. (Invert the top shell to scrape out the organs and excess water.) Remove and discard the feathery lungs attached to the shell above the leg. Twist off the claws and legs, and crack them with a cleaver or mallet. Cut the body into 4 pieces with a cleaver. Place the crab pieces in a colander to drain the excess liquid, then dust with the cornstarch, shaking off the excess.

If your crab is already cooked and cleaned, twist off the claws and legs, and crack them with a cleaver or mallet. Cut the body into 4 pieces. Dust the crab with the cornstarch, shaking off the excess.

Place a wok or stir-fry pan over high heat until hot. Add the oil, swirling to coat the sides. Add the onion, garlic, and ginger and cook, stirring, until fragrant, about 30 seconds. Add the sauce and bring to a boil. Add the crab and cook, stirring, until well mixed. Cover and simmer until the crab is heated through and the sauce thickens, 5 to 7 minutes. Stir in the coconut milk and sesame oil and cook for 1 minute.

Transfer to a serving plate. Garnish with the top shell of the crab, the bell pepper, and green onion and serve.

MAKES 2 SERVINGS

Steamed Crab with Eggplant

This recipe will work with any kind of crab, but I prefer Dungeness or blue crabs when they are in season. I first tasted this dish in Wuzhen, where they cook traditional dishes with locally produced bean paste.

1 ounce dried bean thread noodles

1 whole live or cooked Dungeness crab

SAUCE

1 tbsp. soy sauce

1 tsp. Chinese rice wine or dry sherry

1 tsp. chili bean paste

1 tsp. minced garlic

1 tsp. vegetable oil

2 medium-sized Asian eggplants, cut lengthwise into ½-inch-thick slices

⅛ tsp. salt

2 sprigs cilantro

1 green onion, green part only, julienned

¼ red bell pepper, seeded and julienned

1 tsp. Chili Oil (page 58) or store-bought chili oil

In a medium bowl, soak the noodles in warm water to cover until softened, about 15 minutes; drain. Cut the noodles in half crosswise, and set aside.

To cook a live crab, bring a large pot of water to a boil. Slip the crab into the water. Cook for 2 minutes. Drain, then rinse the crab under cold water, and drain again. If you like, pull off the top shell in one piece and reserve for garnish. (Invert the top shell to scrape out the organs.) Remove and discard the feathery lungs attached to the shell above the leg. Twist off the claws and legs, and crack them with a cleaver or mallet. Cut the body into 4 pieces with a cleaver. Place the crab pieces in a colander to drain the excess liquid.

If your crab is already cooked and cleaned, twist off the claws and legs, and crack them with a cleaver or mallet. Cut the body into 4 pieces.

To prepare the sauce, combine the soy sauce, rice wine, hot bean paste, garlic, and oil in a small saucepan and bring to a boil. Set aside.

Prepare a wok or stir-fry pan for steaming (see page 23). Evenly layer the noodles in a shallow, heatproof dish. Season the eggplant with the salt. Fan slices of eggplant evenly over the noodles. Place the dish in the steamer, cover, and steam over high heat until the eggplant is soft, about 5 minutes.

Arrange the crab pieces on top of the eggplant. Pour the sauce over the crab. Cover and continue to steam over high heat until the crab is heated through, about 5 minutes.

Garnish with the top shell of the crab, the cilantro, green onion, and bell pepper. Drizzle chili oil around the plate and serve.

MAKES 4 SERVINGS

NO! THIS IS A CHINESE DISH?!

Cheese? Milk? Wheat pancakes? Baked sweet potatoes? Potato cakes? Edible flowers? Roasted Yak? Wildflower honey? I'll bet you've never seen these foods on the menu of your neighborhood Chinese restaurant. But millions of ethnic Chinese eat them daily. In Yunnan Province's warmer regions, people incorporate fruit and wildflowers into their dishes. As a special treat, grilled cheese is served with a sweet flower syrup. In the mountainous north, too cold for cultivating rice, wild mountain wheat, garlic, and root vegetables are staples. The yak provides dairy products and meat. To prepare for long winters, the native people pickle summer garden vegetables and cure meats, creating smoked jerky, sausages, and bacon. They also hunt wild animals and harvest wild edibles like underwater grass, young tree leaves, tree fungus, and mushrooms. You can't get more organic or fresh than that!

Jade Lobster

Lobster is perfect for festive occasions; I can never get jaded with it. This dish involves cilantro oil, which adds flavor and a lovely jade-green hue. With lobster, I never lose my head or tail. I save them for a decorative presentation or use them later for a big pot of *jook*, my favorite rice porridge.

One 1½-pound live lobster

MARINADE

1 bunch spinach
(about 1 pound),cleaned

2 tbsp. cornstarch

¼ tsp. salt

⅛ tsp. ground white pepper

Vegetable oil for
deep-frying

2 tbsp. minced garlic

1 tbsp. chopped ginger

¼ cup Rich Homemade Broth
(page 49) or canned chicken
broth

3 tbsp. Chinese rice
wine or dry sherry

2 tsp. cornstarch
dissolved in 4 tsp. water

2 tbsp. Cilantro Oil
(page 58)

To prepare the lobster, plunge the lobster, head first, into a pot of rapidly boiling water; cook for 1½ minutes. Lift the lobster from the water and plunge it into an ice bath to stop the cooking process. Cut off the claws and legs with kitchen scissors or a knife. Remove the meat from the claws. Pull the tail off the body with a sharp downward quarter-turn. Cut the tail along the underside with a pair of kitchen shears. Work the lobster meat from the shell. Reserve the head and tail shells for a garnish. Cut all of the lobster meat into 1-inch pieces. Put the pieces into a large bowl and set aside.

To make the marinade, bring a large pot of water to a boil over high heat. Add the spinach and blanch until bright green, about 1 minute. Drain in a colander. Put the spinach into a blender and whirl, adding up to ¼ cup water, if necessary, to make a smooth purée. Pour the spinach purée over the lobster and stir to coat evenly. Let stand for 10 minutes. Lift the lobster from the marinade and transfer to a clean bowl. Sprinkle on the cornstarch, salt, and pepper, tossing to coat evenly.

In a 2-quart saucepan, pour oil to a depth of 2 inches and heat to 360 degrees F on a deep-fry thermometer. Add half of the lobster to the hot oil, and deep-fry until it is cooked through and crispy on the edges, about 2 minutes. Remove with a wire strainer or slotted spoon and drain on paper towels. Repeat with the remaining lobster. Reserve the oil.

Place a wok or stir-fry pan over high heat until hot. Add 2 tablespoons of the reserved oil, swirling to coat the sides. Add the garlic and ginger and cook, stirring, until fragrant, about 10 seconds. Add the broth and wine and bring to a boil. Add the cornstarch mixture and cook, stirring, until the sauce boils and thickens, about 1 minute. Add the lobster pieces and cook until just heated through. Add the cilantro oil and toss to mix. Discard any remaining oil, or strain and save for another use.

Transfer the lobster to a serving plate. Garnish with the lobster head and tail shell and serve.

MAKES 4 SERVINGS

COMING OF AGE

When a girl in the matriarchal Musuo tribe
reaches thirteen, it's time for an important ritual:
her passage from childhood to adulthood.
Accompanied by her maternal uncle, this youngster
entered the matriarch's house dressed in jeans.
Donning a woman's traditional clothing
for the first time, she was transformed
into a beautiful young woman.
Now she would have her own dwelling and full
property rights. She symbolically stood with
one foot on a piece of pork and the other on a bag
of rice, and after paying respects to the gods,
she drank tea with the matriarch. Then, as her first
adult activity, she brought a traditional delicacy,
preserved pork, to the villagers.

Beijing Sweet-and-Sour Spareribs

Because of the popularity of black vinegar in the north, Beijing sweet-and-sour sauce tends to be dark brown and more tangy than sweet. If you don't feel like dealing with bones or don't have a heavy-duty cleaver nearby, you can substitute country-style ribs.

MARINADE

2 eggs, beaten

¼ cup cornstarch

1 tbsp. Chinese rice wine or dry sherry

1 tsp. salt

2 pounds spareribs, cut into 1- to 1½-inch pieces

Vegetable oil for deep-frying

SAUCE

½ cup sugar

¾ cup Chinese black vinegar or balsamic vinegar

2 tbsp. Worcestershire sauce

1 tsp. salt

4 cloves garlic, peeled and minced

1 fresh jalapeño chile, thinly sliced

1 tsp. cornstarch dissolved in 2 tsp. water

To make the marinade, combine the eggs, cornstarch, rice wine, and salt in a large bowl and mix well. Add the spareribs and stir to coat evenly. Let stand for 1 hour, or cover and marinate in the refrigerator overnight.

In a wok, stir-fry pan, or 2-quart saucepan, pour oil to a depth of 2 inches and heat to 350 degrees F on a deep-fry thermometer. Working in batches, deep-fry the spareribs, stirring gently to prevent the pieces from sticking together, until golden brown and crisp, about 10 minutes per batch. Remove with a wire strainer or slotted spoon to paper towels to drain. Carefully pour the oil into a heatproof bowl, reserving the oil.

To make the sauce, combine the sugar, vinegar, Worcestershire sauce, and salt in a small bowl and mix well.

Place a wok or stir-fry pan over high heat until hot. Add 1 tbsp. of the reserved oil, swirling to coat the sides. Add the garlic and chile and cook, stirring, until fragrant, about 20 seconds. Add the sauce and bring to a boil. Add the spareribs and cook until heated through, about 1 minute. Add the cornstarch mixture and boil until the sauce thickens. Discard any remaining oil, or strain and save for another use.

Transfer to a serving plate and serve.

MAKES 4 SERVINGS

DO IT YOURSELF!

What kind of restaurant makes you sweat and toil over a hot grill, cook your own food, and stand up while you work? Step up to the challenge at BBQ King Restaurant in Beijing. This 150-year-old restaurant features super-size, tabletop grills that are as large as dining tables. You choose your ingredients and cook your own specialties. BBQ King is a local landmark, one of the diminishing number of places that represent "old Beijing."

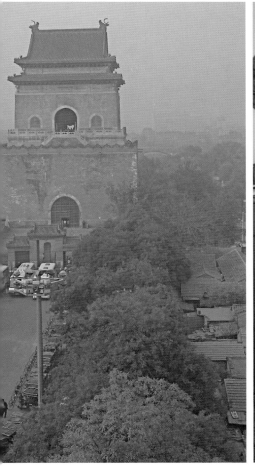

Char Siu with Spicy Pickled Cucumbers

You can find Chinese barbecued pork (*char siu*) in many Chinatown delis, but there's nothing like making your own. The wonderful aroma of roasted *char siu* is so inviting that your dinner guests won't be able to wait for dinner to begin. If you end up with leftover pork (an unlikely scenario if you follow my recipe), save it for wonton soup or Grandma Yan's Signature Fried Rice (page 126).

MARINADE

¼ cup soy sauce

¼ cup honey

¼ cup hoisin sauce

3 tbsp. Chinese rice wine or dry sherry

2 tsp. minced garlic

2 tsp. minced ginger

2 tbsp. sugar

1 tsp. sesame oil

1 tsp. ground white pepper

1 tsp. Chinese five-spice powder

1½ pounds boneless pork butt or other well-marbled pork cut

2 cups Spicy Pickled Cucumbers (page 62)

To make the marinade, combine the soy sauce, honey, hoisin sauce, rice wine, garlic, ginger, sugar, sesame oil, white pepper, and five-spice powder in a large bowl and mix well. Cut the meat into 3 equal pieces. Place in the marinade and turn to coat evenly. Cover and let marinate in the refrigerator for at least 4 hours, or overnight for a richer flavor.

Preheat the oven to 400 degrees F. Place a rack over a foil-lined baking pan. Pour water to a depth of ¼ inch into the pan. Arrange the meat strips in a single layer on the rack, reserving the marinade. Roast, basting the pork with the marinade every 15 minutes and turning the meat over each time, until the pork is no longer pink in the center, about 45 minutes. Allow the meat to rest for 15 minutes before slicing thinly against the grain.

Pour the reserved marinade, along with any pan drippings, into a small saucepan and bring to a boil over high heat. Remove from the heat.

Transfer the pork to a serving plate, alternating slices of pork with pickled cucumbers. Brush the heated marinade over the top and serve.

MAKES 4 SERVINGS

TRADITIONS

I return to China often for business. I look forward to these visits, especially to the southern region where I grew up. When I get swept up in fond memories, my old childhood friends chide me: "Martin, don't dwell in the past; you've moved on!" But, to me, these sojourns serve a greater purpose. I strongly believe that in order for us to have a clear direction in life, we need to appreciate our history.

In the traditional neighborhoods of China's great cities, and in its many rural communities, like my grandfather's village of Kai Ping, I see people who dress and behave as if time has stood still. I'm reminded, again and again, that no matter how quickly China is transforming in this technological age, the Chinese like to maintain tradition. My own love for tradition has never wavered.

Red-Cooked Pork

No, "red cooking" does not mean there's a cook in the kitchen named Red. It's a cooking method, native to Shanghai, which involves simmering food in a combination of sugar and soy sauce. Some "red" sauces, passed down from generations of cooks, are over one hundred years old! Today, every region of China has its variation on red cooking. In Southern China, the sauce is more savory, while in Shanghai, it's sweeter. This recipe is the Shanghai version.

MARINADE

2 tbsp. dark soy sauce

3 tbsp. light soy sauce

½ tsp. Chinese five-spice powder

1½ pounds boneless pork shoulder or pork belly, cut into 2-inch pieces

3 tbsp. vegetable oil

SAUCE

1 cup Rich Homemade Broth (page 49) or canned chicken broth

½ cup Chinese rice wine or dry sherry

3 tbsp. regular soy sauce

2 tbsp. dark soy sauce

2 tbsp. hoisin sauce

¼ cup packed dark brown sugar

6 quarter-sized slices ginger, lightly crushed

2 whole star anise

3 cloves garlic, peeled

1 cinnamon stick

6 green onions, cut into 2-inch-long pieces

2 carrots, peeled and roll-cut into 1-inch pieces

1 small onion, cut into 6 wedges

8 ounces daikon, cut into 1-inch pieces

To make the marinade, combine the dark and light soy sauces and five-spice powder in a large bowl. Add the pork, stirring to coat. Cover, refrigerate, and marinate for 4 hours or overnight.

Place a wok or stir-fry pan over high heat until hot. Add the oil, swirling to coat the sides. Add half of the pork and cook, turning, until browned on all sides, about 5 minutes. Remove the pork with a slotted spoon to a large clay pot. (If you don't have a clay pot, use a large saucepan with a lid.) Repeat with the remaining pork.

To make the sauce, combine the broth, rice wine, regular and dark soy sauces, hoisin sauce, brown sugar, ginger, star anise, garlic, and cinnamon stick in a medium bowl. Pour the sauce over the pork and add enough water to just cover the pork, about 1 cup.

Place the clay pot over medium heat and bring to a simmer. Reduce the heat to medium-low, cover, and simmer gently until the meat is tender, about 1 hour. Tuck the green onions, carrots, onion, and daikon into the cooking liquid and continue to cook, covered, until the vegetables are soft and the meat is fork-tender, about 30 minutes. Serve from the clay pot, or transfer to a serving plate.

MAKES 4 SERVINGS

Forest Garden Stir-Fry

With trained eyes and a keen nose, you can forage for food in the forest in the same way you would in a vegetable garden. Fresh wood ear mushrooms grow on trees in the wild. Their slightly chewy texture and earthy taste provide great contrast to any stir-fry dish. Far from the forest? No problem; you can forage for dried wood ears in many Asian grocery stores.

2 ounces dried wood ear mushrooms

1 medium-sized cucumber, roll-cut into 1-inch pieces

1 tsp. salt

MARINADE

2 tsp. Chinese rice wine or dry sherry

2 tsp. cornstarch

¼ tsp. salt

⅛ tsp. ground white pepper

8 ounces boneless, skinless chicken breast, thinly sliced

SAUCE

3 tbsp. Rich Homemade Broth (page 49) or canned chicken broth

1 tbsp. Chinese rice wine or dry sherry

1 tbsp. chili bean sauce

1 tbsp. soy sauce

2 tbsp. vegetable oil

2 tsp. minced garlic

2 tsp. minced ginger

1 fresh hot red or green chile, thinly sliced

1 crookneck squash, cut into 1-inch pieces

1 zucchini, cut into 1-inch pieces

In a bowl, soak the dried wood ear mushrooms in warm water to cover until softened, about 30 minutes. Drain, chop coarsely, and set aside. Put the cucumber into a colander. Sprinkle with the salt and toss. Let drain over a plate for 30 minutes. Rinse, drain again, and pat dry. Set aside.

To make the marinade, combine the rice wine, cornstarch, salt, and pepper in a medium bowl and mix well. Add the chicken and stir to coat evenly. Let stand for 10 minutes.

To make the sauce, combine the broth, rice wine, chili bean sauce, and soy sauce in a small bowl and mix well. Set aside.

Place a wok or stir-fry pan over high heat until hot. Add the oil, swirling to coat the sides. Add the garlic, ginger, and chile and cook, stirring, until fragrant, about 10 seconds. Add the chicken and stir-fry until no longer pink, about 2 minutes. Add the squash and zucchini and cook, stirring often, until the zucchini turns bright green, about 1 minute. Add the wood ear mushrooms and the sauce and bring to a boil. Add the cucumber and cook, stirring, until heated through and the sauce thickens, about 2 minutes.

Transfer to a serving plate and serve.

MAKES 4 SERVINGS

Grilled Spiced Pork Chops

Those who live off the land have seasonal diets. Imagination is the key; they create dishes based on what's fresh and available. I am a firm believer in that philosophy. Feel free to experiment with whatever you have on hand. Try chicken breasts instead of pork in this recipe, or home-grown green beans in place of asparagus.

MARINADE

3 tbsp. soy sauce

2 tbsp. honey

1 tbsp. Chinese rice wine or dry sherry

1 tsp. minced ginger

½ tsp. ground black pepper

⅛ tsp. Chinese five-spice powder

4 boneless loin pork chops (each about ½ inch thick)

1 tsp. vegetable oil

12 ounces fresh asparagus

6 fresh shiitake mushrooms, stemmed

SAUCE

¼ cup fresh orange juice

1 tbsp. soy sauce

1 tsp. sesame oil

1 tsp. minced ginger

1 tsp. sugar

⅛ tsp. ground black pepper

¼ tsp. cornstarch dissolved in ½ tsp. water

To make the marinade, combine the soy sauce, honey, rice wine, ginger, pepper, and five-spice powder in a large, wide bowl. Add the pork and stir to coat evenly. Let stand for 30 minutes, or cover and refrigerate for up to 4 hours, turning the pork occasionally.

Place a grill pan over medium-high heat until hot. Brush with the oil. Add the pork chops and cook, turning occasionally, until the meat is no longer pink in the center, about 2 minutes on each side. Transfer to a warm serving platter and cover loosely with foil to keep warm.

Place the asparagus on the grill pan. Cook over medium-high heat, turning occasionally, until tender-crisp, about 3 minutes. Transfer to the platter with the pork. Place the mushroom caps on the grill pan. Cook, turning once, until they are cooked through, about 2 minutes per side. Add to the platter with the pork and asparagus.

To make the sauce, combine the orange juice, soy sauce, sesame oil, ginger, sugar, and pepper in a small saucepan and bring to a boil over medium-high heat. Add the cornstarch mixture and cook, stirring, until the sauce boils and thickens, about 30 seconds.

Pour the sauce over the pork and vegetables and serve.

MAKES 4 SERVINGS

Tangerine Peel Chicken

Instead of peeling a tangerine by hand, why not make this recipe more elegant with segmented fruit. This leaves you with the juiciest part of the flesh and gives the dish a smoother finish. All citrus fruit can be prepared using this technique. Cook this refreshing dish any time of the year, using different citrus fruits when tangerines are not available.

4 pieces dried tangerine peel

2 tangerines

MARINADE

1 egg white, beaten

2 tbsp. cornstarch

1 tsp. Chinese rice wine or dry sherry

¼ tsp. salt

¼ tsp. ground white pepper

1 pound boneless, skinless chicken breast, thinly sliced

SAUCE

¼ cup fresh orange juice

1 tbsp. soy sauce

1 tsp. Chinese rice wine or dry sherry

1 tsp. rice vinegar

1 tsp. sesame oil

4 tsp. sugar

¼ tsp. salt

¼ tsp. ground white pepper

Vegetable oil for deep-frying

8 dried red chiles

One 1-inch piece ginger, peeled and julienned

2 green onions, cut into 2-inch pieces

½ small yellow onion, thinly sliced

1 tsp. cornstarch dissolved in 2 tsp. water

1 tsp. toasted sesame seeds

In a small bowl, soak the dried tangerine peels in warm water to cover until softened, about 20 minutes; drain. Cut into narrow strips and set aside.

Slice off the ends of the tangerines with a knife, hold the fruit with one cut side on the board, and slice downward from top to bottom to remove the peel in strips, working your way around the fruit. Cut deeply enough to remove the white pith. Now turn the tangerine on its side horizontally and cut toward the center of the fruit along each membrane. Slice the fruit segment while leaving the membranes intact. Cut away the white pith from half of the tangerine peels and cut the peels into long, narrow strips. Place the fruit and peels in 2 separate bowls and set aside.

RECIPE CONTINUES ON NEXT PAGE

To make the marinade, combine the egg white, cornstarch, rice wine, salt, and white pepper in a medium bowl and mix well. Add the chicken and stir to coat evenly. Let stand for 10 minutes.

To make the sauce, combine the orange juice, soy sauce, rice wine, vinegar, sesame oil, sugar, salt, and white pepper in a small bowl and stir until the sugar dissolves.

In a 2-quart saucepan, pour oil to a depth of 2 inches and heat to 350 degrees F on a deep-fry thermometer. Lift the chicken from the marinade, drain briefly, and fry, a few pieces at a time, until golden and crisp, about 3 minutes per batch. Remove with a wire strainer or slotted spoon and drain on paper towels. Reserve the oil.

Place a wok or stir-fry pan over high heat until hot. Add 1 tbsp. of the reserved oil, swirling to coat the sides. Add the chiles and ginger and cook, stirring, until fragrant, about 30 seconds. Add the green onions, yellow onion, and the dried and fresh tangerine peels; stir-fry until the onions soften, about 1 minute. Add the sauce and bring to a boil. Add the chicken and tangerine segments and stir to coat with the sauce. Add the cornstarch mixture and cook, stirring, until the sauce boils and thickens, about 30 seconds.

Transfer to a serving plate. Sprinkle the sesame seeds on top and serve.

MAKES 4 SERVINGS

HERE'S TO A FRUITFUL YEAR!

Call them tangerines or Mandarin oranges, by either name they make the perfect housewarming gift. Tote them along when you visit family and friends on Chinese New Year, like gold gems, to symbolically bring them good fortune. Think twice before you throw away the peel. Chinese waste nothing and, traditionally, tangerine peels are dried, salted, and eaten as a snack or throat lozenge or in a variety of dishes. Try this tart treat and pucker up!

Dry-Fried Mongolian Lamb

Leeks are paired with lamb in a classic combination, native to the northern and western regions of China. When I cook with leeks, I rinse them well through several changes of water until the water runs clear. The light, sweet onion flavor is well worth the small amount of effort in preparation.

MARINADE

1 tbsp. light soy sauce

1 tbsp. dark soy sauce

1 tbsp. Chinese rice wine or dry sherry

2 tsp. cornstarch

12 ounces tender boneless lamb from the leg or loin, thinly sliced across the grain

SAUCE

2 tbsp. hoisin sauce

1 tbsp. rice vinegar

1 tbsp. regular soy sauce

1 tsp. dark soy sauce

2 tbsp. vegetable oil

2 tbsp. minced garlic

7 dried red chiles

1 large or 2 small leeks, sliced into 3-inch-long pieces and cut lengthwise into long, thin shreds

¼ red onion, thinly sliced

To make the marinade, combine the light and dark soy sauces, rice wine, and cornstarch in a medium bowl and mix well. Add the lamb and stir to coat evenly. Let stand for 10 minutes.

To make the sauce, combine the hoisin sauce, rice vinegar, and regular and dark soy sauce in a small bowl and mix well.

Place a wok or stir-fry pan over high heat until hot. Add 1 tbsp. of the oil, swirling to coat the sides. Add the lamb and stir-fry until barely pink, 2 to 3 minutes. Remove the meat to a plate and set aside.

Return the wok to high heat and add the remaining 1 tbsp. oil. Add the garlic and chiles and cook, stirring, until fragrant, about 10 seconds. Add the leeks and onion and stir-fry until the leeks are wilted, about 1 minute. Return the meat to the pan. Add the sauce and toss to coat.

Transfer to a serving plate and serve.

MAKES 4 SERVINGS

Panda's Favorite

I thought I knew bamboo shoots until I had them in a simple farmers' market in Chengdu. The local chefs prepared it just right; my whole crew was devouring bamboo shoots like a pack of starving pandas. Since that visit, bamboo shoots have shot up several notches on my veggie meter. I've added turkey to this simple stir-fry for a healthy and balanced meal.

MARINADE

1 tbsp. Chinese rice wine or dry sherry

1 tbsp. soy sauce

2 tsp. cornstarch

12 ounces turkey breast strips or turkey cutlets, thinly sliced

1 tbsp. vegetable oil

1 tsp. minced garlic

6 button mushrooms, thinly sliced

2 green onions, cut into 1-inch pieces

One 8-ounce can whole bamboo shoots, drained and thinly sliced

1 tbsp. chili bean paste

1 tbsp. soy sauce

1 fresh hot red chile, thinly sliced

To make the marinade, combine the rice wine, soy sauce, and cornstarch in a bowl and mix well. Add the turkey and stir to coat evenly. Let stand for 10 minutes.

Place a wok or stir-fry pan over high heat until hot. Add the oil, swirling to coat the sides. Add the garlic and cook, stirring, until fragrant, about 10 seconds. Add the mushrooms and green onions and stir-fry until the mushrooms begin to release their liquid, 1 to 2 minutes. Add the turkey and cook, stirring, until no longer pink, about 2 minutes. Add the bamboo shoots and stir to combine. Add the bean paste and soy sauce and stir until well combined and the bamboo shoots are heated through, about 1 minute more.

Transfer to a serving platter. Garnish with the sliced chile and serve.

MAKES 4 SERVINGS

A BEAR OF AN APPETITE

The giant panda, one of the best-loved endangered species in the world, lives in the Wolong Nature Reserve, high in the remote mountains of Sichuan Province. Here, in their natural habitat, one of the world's largest research centers protects, breeds, and studies them. The center is ensuring that these beautiful animals have a future on their planet— and that they can be enjoyed for many generations to come.

Pandas eat fruit, vegetables, and plenty of bamboo. These guys even have chefs who make them gourmet treats, like super-nutritious cakes. I have cooked for all kinds of people, all over the world . . . but, for me, this was a bear of a cooking assignment! I was really nervous . . . but my new pals were so excited by my cooking, they gave me a great big bear hug. They stuffed themselves, then took a long snooze!

Twice-Cooked Duck

Succulent and delicious, duck is always a crowd-pleaser at Chinese banquets. The two different ways of cooking the duck in this dish result in a contrasting moist cooked interior and nice, crispy exterior. I like to serve Mandarin pancakes or flour tortillas with the duck. Combine them to make duck quesadillas!

One 4- to 6-pound whole duck, halved lengthwise, rinsed, and wing tips removed

POACHING LIQUID

One 1-inch-long piece ginger, peeled and thinly sliced

3 cloves garlic, peeled and thinly sliced

6 whole star anise

3 pieces dried tangerine peel

2 cinnamon sticks

1½ tsp. toasted Sichuan peppercorns

4 cardamom pods, lightly crushed

⅛ tsp. black peppercorns, lightly crushed

1½ cups soy sauce

Vegetable oil for deep-frying

Mandarin pancakes or small flour tortillas for serving

½ English cucumber, julienned

5 green onions, julienned

¼ cup hoisin sauce

To poach the duck, place the duck halves, skin side up, in a 5-quart pot and pour in enough cold water to just cover (about 4 cups). Add the ginger, garlic, star anise, tangerine peel, cinnamon sticks, Sichuan peppercorns, cardamom pods, black peppercorns, and soy sauce. Bring to a boil over high heat. Reduce the heat to medium-low, cover, and simmer gently until the duck is just cooked through, about 30 minutes.

Carefully lift the duck from the poaching liquid with a large wire skimmer and transfer to a colander or wire rack, skin side up, to drain. Let cool to room temperature. Save the poaching liquid for another use. Working with one duck half at a time, use a boning knife to carefully remove the breast meat from the breastbone, keeping the breast meat attached to the thigh. You will have 2 duck halves, each with a boneless breast attached to a bone-in thigh.

Pour oil into a wok, stir-fry pan, or large, deep skillet to a depth of 2 inches and heat to 350 degrees F on a deep-fry thermometer. Working with one half at a time, deep-fry the duck until the skin is golden brown and crispy, 5 to 6 minutes. Drain the duck on paper towels. Carve the duck, including the crisp skin, into thin slices.

Transfer the duck to a serving plate. Serve with the pancakes and small bowls of the cucumber, green onions, and hoisin sauce on the side.

MAKES 4 SERVINGS

SOME LIKE IT HOT

Not all hot pots are created equal. Mongolian,
Beijing, Sichuan, or Cantonese, each hot pot
comes with its unique style, spices, and ingredients.
Whichever style you prefer, it's a fun way for
families and friends to share a delicious meal.
Another great thing about hot pots: there are never
too many cooks to spoil the broth. "Hot-potting"
is totally interactive, and the broth only gets
richer with more added ingredients.
The more the merrier!

Sichuan Hot Pot

In Sichuan, hot pots come in two flavors: hot or burn-the-house-down hot. While the rest of China uses a light, savory broth, the people of Sichuan use a broth that's heavily laced with dried chiles, hot chili oil, and chili sauce. For this recipe, I took a more moderate approach. Feel free to "add fuel to the fire" at your own peril.

BROTH

6 cups Rich Homemade Broth (page 49) or canned chicken broth

2 quarter-sized slices ginger, lightly crushed

2 green onions, halved crosswise and lightly crushed

6 whole dried chiles

2 ounces dried bean thread noodles

2 pounds tender boneless beef

One 14-ounce package firm tofu, drained

2 pounds mixed leafy green vegetables, such as bok choy, spinach, and napa cabbage

SESAME DIPPING SAUCE

½ cup soy sauce

3 tbsp. Rich Homemade Broth (page 49) or canned chicken broth

1 tbsp. sesame seed paste or chunky peanut butter

1 tbsp. sesame oil

½ cup Chef Yan's Chili Sauce (page 56)

½ cup Mustard Dipping Sauce (page 52)

To prepare the broth, combine the broth, ginger, green onions, and chiles in a large pot and bring to a boil over high heat. Reduce the heat to medium-low, cover, and simmer for 30 minutes. Remove and discard the ginger and green onions. Keep broth warm over low heat.

In a medium bowl, soak the noodles in warm water to cover until softened, about 15 minutes. Drain. Using a pair of kitchen shears, cut the noodles into 4-inch-long pieces.

Cut the beef into thin slices across the grain. Cut the tofu into 1-inch cubes; drain. Cut the vegetables into bite-sized pieces. Arrange the noodles, beef, tofu, and vegetables on a large platter. Cover and refrigerate until ready to cook.

To make the sesame dipping sauce, combine the soy sauce, broth, sesame seed paste, and sesame oil in a small bowl and mix well.

Set a hot pot or an electric wok in the center of the table. Pour the broth into the hot pot and add the noodles. Adjust the heat so the broth is gently simmering. Each diner cooks his or her choice of ingredients in the broth. Serve with the 3 dipping sauces on the side.

MAKES 8 SERVINGS

Living History

An American friend of mine has been living in Beijing for a year. He recently told me, "The summer here is too hot, the winter too cold. This is a hard city to like, but an easy city to love." What my friend found out in twelve months took me more than twelve years to realize. Beijing is a hard city to like, but boy, do I love it!

As a world economic force, Beijing is a relative newcomer on the scene. For centuries, it was the seat of China's imperial power. Today, Beijing is in the spotlight as a city of commerce, a fast-evolving international player.

Yet despite its imperial grandeur, its stately edifices, wide boulevards, and sky-reaching glass towers, Beijing is a very Chinese city, one with old temples, open-air markets, and neighborhood teahouses. Beijing people are down-to-earth, hardworking, and no-nonsense. In Shanghai and Hong Kong, you may find keener fashion sense and more international restaurants, but in Beijing, you find the engine that keeps the country going.

Let's not disregard all the art and culture that the city has to offer. I can spend days at the Museum of the Forbidden City, looking at thousands of artifacts dating from the Bronze and Stone Ages to modern times. A short trip from the city is the Great Wall, considered

one of the seven wonders of the world. And for a bit of living history, you can visit the Hutong, an age-old district inhabited by the same families for generations upon generations.

Beijing's regal and sophisticated cuisine originated in the days of the Imperial Court. Top chefs from the far reaches of the country would gather there for the privilege of cooking for emperors, literati, officials, and visiting dignitaries. These chefs contributed the best of their regional cooking styles and their local flavors, resulting in a cuisine that possesses an extraordinary range of wonderful dishes.

My favorite Beijing dining scene is far from the Forbidden City, however. I love visiting small, home-style eateries in old neighborhoods, for their wonderful comfort food, still prepared according to recipes handed down for generations. Even in the middle of one of Beijing's harsh, cold winters, you will find me beating the pavement in the Hutong, looking for my favorite wheat noodles, steamed buns, and meat dumplings. Or maybe it's meat and vegetables in large, thin pancakes or Muslim Barbecue on bamboo skewers. For me, these delicacies will always be the most endearing part about this city that's too hot in the summer and too cold in the winter.

New Beijing Lamb

Because Beijing is close to Mongolia, you can find lamb and mutton (lamb that's more than a year old) in most of the city's restaurants, as well as at curbside food stands. As a new mutton convert, I cook it with lots of garlic and ginger and serve it with strong condiments like vinegar, chili sauce, rice wine, and hoisin sauce.

MARINADE

3 tbsp. soy sauce

1 tbsp. Chinese rice wine or dry sherry

1 tsp. minced garlic

1 tsp. cornstarch

¼ tsp. ground black pepper

1 rack of lamb, cut into double chops (at least 8 chops total)

HOISIN-GARLIC DIPPING SAUCE

1 tbsp. hoisin sauce

1½ tsp. sesame oil

1 tsp. chili garlic sauce

¼ tsp. minced garlic

¼ tsp. minced ginger

1 tsp. vegetable oil

Soy-Vinegar Dipping Sauce (page 52)

Beijing Dipping Sauce (page 53)

To make the marinade, combine the soy sauce, rice wine, garlic, cornstarch, and pepper in a large bowl and mix well. Add the lamb chops and stir to coat evenly. Let marinate for 1 to 2 hours.

To make the hoisin-garlic dipping sauce, combine the hoisin sauce, sesame oil, chili garlic sauce, garlic, and ginger in a bowl and mix well. Set aside.

Place a grill pan over medium-high heat until hot. Brush with the oil. Place the chops on the grill pan and cook, turning once, until medium-rare, about 3 minutes on each side.

Transfer the lamb chops to a serving plate and serve with the 3 dipping sauces on the side.

MAKES 4 SERVINGS

Shangri-la Beef

The original recipe for this dish featured yaks, which are long-haired highland buffalo. Seeing that yak meat is hard to find, I recommend beef steak as a substitute. The dry-frying technique is designed to bring out the beef's more concentrated flavors.

MARINADE

1 tbsp. regular soy sauce

1 tbsp. dark soy sauce

1 tbsp. Chinese rice wine or dry sherry

1 tbsp. cornstarch

12 ounces beef tri-tip or flank steak, thinly sliced across the grain

2 tbsp. vegetable oil

14 dried red chiles

2 tbsp. minced garlic

4 green onions, cut into 2-inch pieces

¼ red bell pepper, seeded and cut into long, narrow strips

1 tbsp. chili bean paste

1 tbsp. hoisin sauce

To make the marinade, combine the regular and dark soy sauces, rice wine, and cornstarch in a medium bowl and mix well. Add the beef and stir to coat evenly. Let stand for 10 minutes.

Place a wok or stir-fry pan over high heat until hot. Add the oil, swirling to coat the sides. Add the chiles and garlic and cook, stirring, until fragrant, about 20 seconds. Add the beef and stir-fry until barely pink in the center, 3 to 4 minutes. Add the green onions and bell pepper and cook until the green onions wilt. Add the chili bean paste and hoisin sauce and toss to coat the meat evenly.

Transfer to a serving plate and serve.

MAKES 4 SERVINGS

Shangri-la: A Lost Eden

Ever since British author James Hilton wrote *Lost Horizon*, a novel that turned Buddhist accounts of a physical dimension accessible only to the enlightened into a Western tale of a lost Eden, travelers have come searching for "Shangri-la."

Well, I found a beautiful town named Shangri-la on the border of northern Yunnan Province in southwestern China, and it's as close to paradise as I can imagine! Upon arrival, I saw yaks peacefully munching acres of wild mountain wheat. Peace is the word that best describes Shangri-la, a center of Tibetan Buddhist learning and pilgrimage. Approaching pilgrims are guided by the impressive façade of Songzanlin Si Temple, which, at eleven thousand feet, towers over Shangri-la. This monastery, built in the 1600s, has been the center of Tibetan Buddhism in Yunnan Province for centuries. Golden figures of Buddha, decorating its exterior, give the building an extraordinary aura, especially at sunset. The view of surrounding snowcapped peaks from atop the monastery is awe-inspiring. Hundreds of steps lead up to the main entrance, so, in addition to strong faith, the seven hundred–plus resident monks must have strong legs! It's an honor for a family to have a son admitted to the temple. Here, young boys receive their education as well as spiritual guidance.

Walking along cobblestone streets, you find homes three or four stories high. Live animals and wheat, preserved meats, and homemade cheeses are stored on the first level. Prized Pu'er tea is stored on the second level, in the kitchen and living room. The prayer room and bedrooms are located above, on one or two more floors.

In this age of mass communication, tribal people are no longer as isolated; many young people now speak Mandarin, as well as their local dialect. I befriended one sophisticated native, Bai Ma, who left at a young age to pursue a successful television career in Beijing. Now, years later, he's returned to run a hotel and restaurant. Lucky me— I scored a delicious meal and a personal tour.

Among the most popular dishes in Shangri-la are grilled yak and leg of lamb, fried lamb ribs, eggplant, tomatoes, fried potato pancakes, crispy potato dumplings, eight treasures rice, and rice noodles. Locals consider it a special treat to order a bowl of noodles at a small corner eatery. The earthenware cooking pots used here are made of an unusual clay that turns jet black when fired.

On Bai Ma's tour, we passed many prayer flags, or *dar cho*, inscribed with Buddhist scripture, and they released blessings into the universe to benefit all humankind as they fluttered in the breeze. Everywhere, you see prayer wheels, including one of the biggest in the world! Bai Ma said it contained passages of Buddhist scripture. Whenever it makes a complete turn, blessings go out to the world. It takes a lot of power to turn the huge wheel, but that means it sends out very powerful blessings, hopefully bringing world harmony closer. For the kids of Shangri-la, it's the local merry-go-round—and that's a blessing, too!

Dragon and Lion Head Meatballs

Lion head meatballs is a classic dish in Shanghai. I've added shrimp mousse to represent the dragon inside the lion head, and lightened the dish by replacing the traditional pork fat with soft tofu. Don't worry: The king of beasts is keeping his mane (napa cabbage) and still has plenty of bite.

LION'S HEAD

1½ pounds ground beef

¼ cup Shrimp Mousse (page 64)

2 green onions, finely chopped

2 quarter-sized slices ginger, minced

3 tbsp. cornstarch

2 tbsp. Chinese rice wine or dry sherry

2 tbsp. dark soy sauce

1 tsp. Chinese five-spice powder

1 tsp. salt

1 tsp. ground white pepper

DRAGON'S HEAD

¼ cup Shrimp Mousse, chilled

Vegetable oil for deep-frying

1 head napa cabbage, quartered lengthwise

1 tsp. salt

2 cups Rich Homemade Broth (page 49) or canned chicken broth

2 green onions, chopped

2 quarter-sized slices ginger, lightly crushed

1 tsp. chili garlic sauce

1 tbsp. cornstarch dissolved in 2 tbsp. water

1 tsp. toasted sesame seeds

To prepare the lion's head, combine the ground beef, shrimp mousse, green onions, ginger, cornstarch, rice wine, soy sauce, five-spice powder, salt, and white pepper in the bowl of an electric mixer. Using the paddle attachment, mix on medium speed until the mixture is homogeneous and stiff. Divide into 8 equal portions. With wet hands, roll each portion into a ball. Flatten each ball to a 4-inch disk.

For the dragon's head, divide the shrimp mousse into 8 equal portions. With wet hands, roll each portion into a ball.

Put one shrimp ball in the center of each meat disk and fold the meat up and over the shrimp, completely encasing the shrimp ball. Shape into a ball. Transfer to a lightly oiled plate and set aside.

RECIPE CONTINUES ON NEXT PAGE

In a wok or stir-fry pan, pour the oil to a depth of 1 inch and heat to 350 degrees F on a deep-fry thermometer. Working with a few at a time, deep-fry the meatballs until deep golden brown, about 3 minutes. Lift the meatballs out with a wire strainer or a slotted spoon. Drain on paper towels. Carefully pour the oil into a heatproof bowl, reserving the oil.

Place a clean wok or stir-fry pan over high heat. Add 1 tbsp. of the reserved oil, swirling to coat the sides. Add the cabbage and salt and cook, stirring, until the cabbage is lightly wilted, about 30 seconds. Arrange the meatballs on top of the cabbage. Add the broth, half of the green onions, and the ginger and bring to a boil. Cover, reduce the heat to medium, and simmer until the meatballs are cooked through and the cabbage is tender, about 15 minutes.

Add the chili garlic sauce, then add the cornstarch mixture. Cook, stirring, until the sauce boils and thickens.

Transfer the cabbage to a serving platter and arrange the meatballs on top. Spoon the sauce over the meatballs and garnish with the sesame seeds and remaining green onions and serve.

MAKES 8 MEATBALLS, ABOUT 8 SERVINGS

I AM MEATBALL, HEAR ME ROAR!

Hair ball caught in your throat? No, it's not from your lion's head meatball. This creation owes its name to a creative chef who was inspired by an ancient sculpture of a male lion with a large head atop a compact body. Traditional lion's heads come in a set of four, one for each of the four seasons. The cabbage represents the lion's mane. The dish is also known as "happiness meatballs," because it symbolizes an abundance of happiness, good fortune, and health.

Wine-Poached Chicken

In Shanghai, one of the most popular dishes is "drunken chicken," which leads to the question: What's the legal alcohol limit for adult chickens? This is a perfect main course that can also be served as an appetizer. It goes especially well with beer or wine. For this recipe, I suggest using top-of-the-line Shaoxing wine from Shanxi, China. Caution: Don't poach and drive.

POACHING LIQUID

3 quarter-sized slices ginger, lightly crushed

2 whole green onions

2 whole star anise

1 cinnamon stick

1 tbsp. soy sauce

1 tbsp. Chinese rice wine or dry sherry

2 tbsp. salt

2 tbsp. sugar

4 boneless, skin-on chicken breast halves

MARINADE

2 cups Rich Homemade Broth (page 49), or, reserved poaching liquid

¼ cup Chinese rice wine or dry sherry

2 tsp. salt

½ tsp. sugar

To make the poaching liquid, combine the ginger, green onions, star anise, cinnamon stick, soy sauce, rice wine, salt, and sugar in a large pot. Add the chicken and enough water to just cover (about 3 cups). Bring just to a boil over medium-high heat, then reduce the heat to medium-low and simmer gently for 10 minutes. Remove the pot from the heat, cover, and set aside, undisturbed, until the poaching liquid is completely cool and the chicken is cooked through, about 2 hours.

To make the marinade, combine the broth or reserved poaching liquid, rice wine, salt, and sugar in a medium bowl and stir until the salt and sugar dissolve. Place the meat in a medium nonreactive bowl. Pour the marinade over the chicken and stir gently to completely submerge the chicken. Cover with plastic wrap and refrigerate overnight or for up to 2 days.

Lift the chicken from the marinade and thinly slice the meat. Transfer the meat to a serving platter or line the inside of a small, deep bowl with the skin-on chicken slices. Fill the bowl with the remaining chicken and press down to compact. Place the serving plate face down on top of the bowl to invert the chicken onto the plate. Swiftly flip the bowl and plate to position the plate on the bottom. Carefully lift the bowl off and serve chilled or at room temperature.

MAKES 4 TO 6 SERVINGS

Desserts &
Beverages

Here's a common question from my TV viewers: "Why don't the Chinese have a sweet tooth?" The answer is we do. It's just that Chinese sweets and desserts are not loaded with butter, cream (dairy products are not popular in China), chocolate, and processed sugar. But that is not to say we don't have a sweet tooth. We simply satisfy our cravings for sweets in different ways.

Many classic Chinese desserts use fresh fruits and nuts as their main ingredients. On a recent visit to Western China, I came across a wonderful banana dish. Coated in a crispy sugar syrup, it's crunchy on the outside, soft and moist on the inside, and enticing throughout. This recipe actually dates back hundreds of years, to the Yuan Dynasty. I've updated it as Crispy Glazed Bananas (facing page). Try it and make some dessert history of your own.

Shanxi Province is famous for its dates, as in the edible kind that grows on trees. Naturally the dessert chefs put them to good use. A fine example is the Steamed Date Buns on page 215. Master this dish and you will never be dateless.

With increased international exposure, China is adapting many foriegn culinary tastes and habits. On the dessert table, I've witnessed a surge in the popularity of ice cream and cakes. The Fresh Ginger Ice Cream on page 208 captures this trend and combines it with a traditional Chinese ingredient—ginger. In Southern China, lychees and mangoes have been crowd-pleasing fruits for ages. I pay tribute to both with my rendition of Lychee Pudding with Strawberry Sauce (page 210) and Mango Purée with Coconut Milk (page 204).

From time to time in my travels, I come across interesting and memorable beverages. Almond milk (page 218) is something that I grew up with in Guangzhou, and so is *ba pao cha*, Chinese Sweet Iced Tea (page 220). Ginseng tea used to be a beverage served only in the wealthiest of households. I modified the recipe, adding lemongrass (Lemongrass Tea with Ginseng, page 224), to make it a beverage we can all enjoy every day.

What's a perfect ending to a Chinese meal? Try any of the recipes in this chapter and find a sweet surprise.

Crispy Glazed Bananas

In North America, a classic is anything that transcends one generation. By that definition, this dish is a classic times a hundred! My friends in Western China tell me that this recipe dates back to the Yuan Dynasty (A.D. 1279–1368), and it really got people to "go bananas" during the Qing Dynasty (A.D. 1644–1911). How's that for a taste of history?

SAUCE	BATTER	
1 cup packed brown sugar	⅔ cup all-purpose flour	4 firm, ripe bananas
½-inch piece ginger, lightly crushed	¼ cup cornstarch	4 scoops Fresh Ginger Ice Cream (page 208)
½ cup water	½ tsp. baking powder	
	½ tsp. salt	
	¾ cup water	
Vegetable oil for deep-frying	1½ tsp. vegetable oil	

To make the sauce, combine the brown sugar, ginger, and water in a small saucepan and cook over medium heat, stirring, until the sugar dissolves and the sauce thickens slightly, about 5 minutes. Keep warm over low heat.

In a 2-quart saucepan, pour oil to a depth of 2 inches and heat to 350 degrees F on a deep-fry thermometer.

Meanwhile, make the batter by combining the flour, cornstarch, baking powder, and salt in a medium bowl. Gradually pour in the water and oil, whisking until the batter is smooth.

Peel the bananas, halve them lengthwise, and then cut in half crosswise. One at a time, dip the bananas into the batter; drain briefly. As the bananas are coated, add them to the hot oil, a few at a time, and deep-fry, turning once, until golden brown, about 3 minutes per batch. Remove with a wire strainer or slotted spoon and drain on paper towels.

To assemble each dessert, place a scoop of ice cream in a bowl, top with 4 crispy bananas, and drizzle one-fourth of the sauce over the top.

MAKES 4 SERVINGS

Mango Purée with Coconut Milk

This wonderful dessert can double as a poolside cocktail . . . or should I call it a refreshing drink rich enough to be a dessert? Either way, serving this concoction in a coconut shell is an elegant idea for home entertaining. My mangoes of choice are the Filipino variety, which are smooth, sweet, and less fibrous. Mexican mangoes are bigger and meatier, and more easily available in North America.

SYRUP

¼ cup sugar

1 cup water

4 medium to large mangoes, peeled, pitted, and cut into cubes

½ cup canned unsweet-ened coconut milk

4 young coconuts, for serving bowls (optional)

To make the syrup, combine the sugar and water in a saucepan. Cook over medium heat, stirring, until the sugar dissolves. Let the syrup cool. Chill until ready to use.

In a blender, combine the mangoes, coconut milk, and syrup; whirl until smooth. Transfer the purée to a pitcher, cover, and chill.

Stir before serving. Serve in coconut bowls, if you like; reserve the coconut water and save some for another use.

MAKES 1 QUART, ABOUT 4 SERVINGS

Five-Spice Flourless Chocolate Cakes

Chocolate is fairly new to Chinese cuisine, but it is wasting no time in gaining new converts, especially in an international metropolis like Shanghai. On a recent visit, I discovered this chocolate delight in one of the city's swanky restaurants and decided to add my personal touch of Chinese five-spice powder.

4 tbsp. butter, melted and kept warm

⅓ cup unsweetened cocoa powder

1 cup heavy cream

8 ounces bittersweet chocolate, chopped

¼ cup sugar

1½ tsp. Chinese five-spice powder

8 ounces mascarpone cheese, at room temperature

3 eggs

WHIPPED CREAM

½ cup heavy cream, chilled

2 tsp. sugar

Mixed fresh berries, for garnish

Preheat the oven to 300 degrees F. Generously butter eight 6-ounce ramekins with the melted butter. Dust the bottom and sides of each ramekin with some of the cocoa powder, tapping out the excess. Set the prepared ramekins on a baking sheet and set aside.

To prepare the chocolate, put ½ cup of the heavy cream in a small saucepan and bring just to a boil over medium heat. Set aside. Combine the chocolate, sugar, and five-spice powder in a large, heat-proof bowl. Set the bowl over a pot of gently simmering water and cook, stirring, until the chocolate is completely melted, about 5 minutes. Add the heated cream to the melted chocolate and mix well. Remove the bowl from the heat and set aside to cool.

To prepare the cakes, combine the mascarpone and remaining ½ cup heavy cream in a large bowl and beat with an electric mixer until smooth. Add the eggs, one at a time, beating well after each addition. Add the chocolate mixture and mix on medium speed until just combined. Do not overmix.

Divide the batter among the 8 prepared ramekins until each is three-fourths full. Bake until the centers are just set, about 1 hour. Remove the cakes from the oven and set aside for 10 minutes before unmolding.

To prepare the whipped cream, beat the heavy cream and sugar together in a large bowl with an electric mixer on high speed until soft peaks form.

Unmold each cake by running a knife around the edge of the cake and inverting it onto a dessert plate. Garnish each cake with a dollop of whipped cream and berries.

MAKES 8 SERVINGS

Fresh Ginger Ice Cream

The Chinese believe that ginger has health-promoting properties and settles the stomach. They will use it in anything. If you try this recipe, I assure you that this unusual and delicious ice cream will waste no time settling in your tummy.

2 cups heavy cream	8 egg yolks
2 cups whole milk	¾ cup sugar
¼ cup grated fresh ginger	
Pinch of salt	

In a heavy saucepan, combine the cream, milk, ginger, and salt and heat over medium heat until bubbles form around the edge of the pan. Remove from the heat and set aside to let steep for 20 minutes.

Using an electric mixer, whisk the egg yolks and sugar together in a medium bowl until pale yellow, about 5 minutes. Slowly add 2 cups of the hot cream mixture, whisking constantly to prevent the eggs from curdling, then pour the mixture back into the saucepan. Cook over low heat, stirring constantly, until the custard is thick enough to coat the back of a wooden spoon, 6 to 8 minutes. Pour the custard through a fine-mesh strainer into a clean mixing bowl, discarding the solids. Cover with plastic wrap and refrigerate until chilled, at least 3 hours.

Pour the custard into an ice cream machine and process according to the manufacturer's directions. Scoop the ice cream into dessert cups and serve.

MAKES 6 TO 8 SERVINGS

Lychee Pudding with Strawberry Sauce

Summer is lychee season in Southern China. One recent summer there was a spectacular harvest, and I found lychees for sale on practically every street corner of Guangzhou. My friends hosted lychee banquets and gave bunches of them to overseas visitors, like me. What do you do with so many fresh lychees? Make pudding! Since lychees are available for only a few weeks out of the year, this recipe calls for the canned variety, which is available year-round. Your guests won't mind, and your lychees won't tell.

1 packet (¼ ounce) powdered unflavored gelatin

3 tbsp. cold water

Two 14-ounce cans lychees in syrup

1½ cups buttermilk

½ tsp. vanilla extract

1 cup heavy cream

¼ cup sugar

SAUCE

1 pint fresh strawberries, hulled, or 1½ cups thawed frozen strawberries

1 tbsp. sugar

1 tbsp. freshly squeezed lemon juice

In a large bowl, sprinkle the gelatin over the cold water and set aside for 5 minutes.

Meanwhile, drain the lychees, reserving ¼ cup of the canning syrup, and transfer them to a blender. Whirl until smooth, then strain through a fine-mesh sieve into a medium bowl, pressing on the solids with the back of a spoon. Discard the solids. Add the buttermilk and vanilla and whisk.

In a small saucepan, combine the cream, sugar, and reserved ¼ cup syrup. Heat over medium heat, stirring occasionally, until bubbles just form around the edge of the pan. Pour the hot cream mixture over the gelatin and stir until the gelatin dissolves. Add the buttermilk mixture and stir until well mixed.

Pour the mixture into 6 dessert cups and refrigerate until set, about 2 hours.

To make the sauce, combine the strawberries, sugar, and lemon juice in a blender. Whirl until smooth. Transfer to a small pitcher and refrigerate until ready to serve.

Serve the puddings chilled, with some of the sauce poured over each.

MAKES 6 SERVINGS

Steamed Ginger Sponge Cake

If you stop and think about its name, sponge cake doesn't sound very appetizing. I guess this is a case in which you can't judge a dessert by its name. Because it's steamed instead of baked, this cake is light as air, and its delicate ginger flavor will make you beg for seconds, and thirds.

Three 2-inch-long pieces ginger, peeled	½ cup vegetable oil	8 eggs
	½ tsp. vanilla extract	3⅓ cups cake flour, sifted
One 14-ounce can unsweetened coconut milk	2 cups sugar	1 tbsp. baking powder

Line a 9-inch round cake pan with parchment paper and grease lightly. Set aside.

Prepare a wok or stir-fry pan for steaming (see page 23).

Using the fine holes of a box grater, grate the ginger into a small bowl. Press the grated ginger through a fine-mesh strainer, pressing on the solids with the back of a spoon, into a liquid measuring cup. Extract enough ginger juice to make ⅓ cup. Discard the solids.

In a small bowl, combine the coconut milk, oil, and vanilla, stirring until well mixed.

In a large bowl, beat together the sugar and eggs with an electric mixer on high speed until pale yellow, about 5 minutes. Slowly add the coconut milk–oil mixture, beating constantly until well mixed. Add the flour and beat on low speed until just combined, about 2 minutes.

Add the baking powder to the ginger juice, stirring once, then immediately add to the batter; beat on medium speed until just mixed.

Pour the batter into the prepared cake pan. Set the pan in the steamer basket, cover, and steam over high heat until the cake is light and fluffy, about 1 hour. Check the water level every 15 minutes and add water to the wok or stir-fry pan if necessary. The cake is done when a toothpick inserted in the center comes out clean.

Invert the cake onto a cake plate and peel off the parchment paper. Serve the cake warm or at room temperature.

MAKES ONE 9-INCH CAKE

Nourishing Our Imagination

It's been said that art (*yishu*) is food for the senses. By that definition, China has a ravenous appetite, and it is a well-fed nation. In Asia, the very act of creating art is considered an art in itself, attended by time-honored techniques and procedures. Aesthetics is built into every action, even the most common aspects of our lives. Perfection is achieved by elevating aesthetics to its highest form, and in doing so, creating a great work of art.

Chinese ceramics, handicrafts, and folk arts, such as paper cutting, embroidery, and puppetry, infuse daily life. Legend has it that shadow theatre (*pi ying xi*), a type of puppetry, began when, during the Han Dynasty, the grief-stricken Emperor Wu ordered attendants to bring his beloved concubine back to life. To simulate her shadowy shape in motion, they manipulated a stick figure, cut from donkey leather, behind a screen of mulberry paper, lit by an oil lamp. They failed to revive the concubine but did give birth to a new art form. Enlivened by opera music, shadow theatre became choice entertainment, especially for invading Mongolian troops, who spread it far and wide.

Since the establishment of the first opera school, Liyuan (Pear Garden), Chinese opera stars have been called "disciples of the pear garden." One of the world's oldest performance arts, beloved by officials and the public, Chinese opera incorporates many art forms, including music, script writing, and scenery, costume, and mask design.

Traditional Chinese music dates back three thousand years, to the Zhou Dynasty. String, wind, and percussion instruments were divided into eight categories, according to the material they were made from: silk, bamboo, wood, stone, metal, clay, gourd, and hide. Orchestras did not have conductors but performed flawlessly before the Imperial Court. With no musical scores, complete memorization was required.

Nowadays, elders enjoy *yayue* (elegant music) from imperial times or *guoyue* (national music), modernized traditional music, while youngsters listen to C-pop, either Cantonese Cantopop or Mandarin Mandopop.

Chinese calligraphy, long a revered art form, consists of harmonious expressions of characters created with brush and ink on silk or paper. Throughout history, famous calligraphers were considered grand masters, as well known as famous brush painters. Their works were highly sought after by the Imperial Court and wealthy patrons.

Classical Chinese ink painting used tools and methods similar to those used in calligraphy. With the aim of moving past the old ways, post–World War II China sent young artists abroad to study Western oil painting. But a popular effort to preserve classical arts, the One Hundred Flowers Campaign, revived traditional ink painting. Today, electrifying Chinese paintings and multimedia artworks draw on both Chinese and Western techniques.

An intricate eye for detail is also needed in the culinary art of food carving. A Chinese tradition passed down through generations, it's now generating worldwide interest. Carrots, papaya, pumpkins, watermelons, taro, turnips, winter melons, radishes, and pineapples are transformed into teapots, baskets, flowers, mythical figures, animals, or even landscapes. Many designs are as old as the art itself. All that's needed is a set of carving knives, a few scoops, steady hands, a lot of concentration . . . and practice, practice, practice.

All art is food for the senses. But in edible art, a true masterpiece must not only be created in good taste, it must taste good!

NO BUN IN THE OVEN

Order a bun in China, and you may not get what you expect. Early Chinese lacked ovens, so traditional buns were steamed instead of baked. They originated in the north, where wheat is cultivated. Now popular everywhere, they are filled with sweet pastes or meats like barbecue pork.

If you're ever in Hong Kong, get your buns over to the annual four-day Cheung Chau Bun Festival. Climb the five-story bun tower and gather as many buns as you can along the way. If you become the bun champion, you can tell your friends at home that China honored you for your buns!

Steamed Date Buns

Shanxi is one of the sweetest spots in China. The reason? Dates, the fruity kind. Local chefs use them in soups, main dishes, and desserts. In this date bun delicacy, the dough is studded with dates and the buns are filled with red bean paste. Now that's my idea of a sweet date treat!

12 dried Chinese red dates

3 tbsp. granulated sugar

1½ tsp. dried yeast

¾ cup warm water

2 cups plus 2 tbsp. all-purpose flour, sifted

1 tbsp. lard or vegetable shortening, melted

5 tbsp. canned red bean paste

2 tbsp. water

ICING

½ cup sweetened condensed milk

3 tbsp. confectioners' sugar

In a medium bowl, soak the dates in warm water to cover until softened, about 30 minutes. Drain; pick through the dates and discard any seeds. Mince the dates and set aside.

In a large mixing bowl, combine the sugar, yeast, and ¾ cup warm water, stirring until the sugar dissolves. Set aside in a warm place until the mixture is foamy on top, about 10 minutes. Add the flour and lard and stir with a wooden spoon until a loose dough forms. Add the dates and knead until evenly distributed. Turn the dough out onto a lightly floured work surface and knead until smooth and elastic, about 10 minutes. Transfer the dough to a large, clean bowl, cover, and set aside in a warm place to rise until doubled in size, about 30 minutes.

Meanwhile, combine the red bean paste and 2 tbsp. water in a small bowl and mix to a smooth, spreadable paste. Set aside.

Turn the dough out onto a lightly floured work surface and roll into a 10-by-14-inch rectangle. Turn the dough so that the short end is facing you. Spread the bean paste over the surface of the dough, leaving a 1½-inch border. Lift the edge of the dough closest to you and roll it up and over the filling, continuing to roll until you reach the end. Pinch the seam shut.

Place the roll, seam side down, on a clean work surface. Using a sharp knife, cut the roll into 12 equal slices. (Cut it in half, then cut each half in half again to make 4 equal pieces. Cut each piece into 3 equal-sized rolls, making 12 rolls.)

Line 2 steamer baskets with parchment paper, cut to fit. Lightly oil the parchment paper. Arrange 6 of the rolls, barely touching, in each prepared basket. Cover each basket with the lid and set aside in a warm place until the rolls double in size, 15 to 20 minutes.

Prepare a wok or stir-fry pan for steaming (see page 23). Stack the steamer baskets and place over simmering water. Steam, covered, until the buns are light and fluffy, 10 to 15 minutes.

To make the icing, combine the condensed milk and confectioners' sugar in a bowl.

Drizzle the icing over the buns and serve warm.

MAKES 12 BUNS

Sweet Potato Croquettes

Do sweet potatoes taste better at higher altitudes? I don't know, but these croquettes tasted absolutely heavenly in Shangri-la. Luckily for me, the recipe travels, so whenever I am in the mood to rekindle my *Lost Horizon* frame of mind, I fry up a new batch of croquettes.

DOUGH

1 pound sweet potatoes

1 egg, lightly beaten

3 tbsp. all-purpose flour

2 tbsp. chopped roasted, salted peanuts

1 tsp. sugar

⅛ tsp. salt

3 cups vegetable oil for deep-frying

2 cups panko (Japanese breadcrumbs)

6 tbsp. unsweetened desiccated coconut

2 eggs

SAUCE

1 cup canned unsweetened coconut milk

2 tbsp. sugar

Pinch of salt

To make the dough, preheat the oven to 400 degrees F. Roast the sweet potatoes on a baking sheet until soft when pierced with the tip of a sharp knife, about 45 minutes. Remove the potatoes from the oven and set aside until cool, then peel and transfer them to a medium bowl. Using a potato masher, coarsely mash the potatoes. Add the egg, flour, peanuts, sugar, and salt and mash until the dough is smooth. Divide the dough into 12 equal portions, then, using wet hands, roll each portion into a walnut-sized ball. Arrange the dough balls, without crowding, on a lightly greased plate.

Pour the oil into a 2-quart saucepan; it should reach a depth of 2 inches. Heat to 350 degrees F on a deep-fry thermometer. Mix the panko and coconut in a shallow bowl. Lightly beat the eggs in a second shallow bowl. One at a time, dip the potato balls into the egg, drain briefly, and then coat with the panko mixture. As the croquettes are coated, add them to the hot oil, a few at a time, and deep-fry, turning occasionally, until golden brown and crisp, about 5 minutes per batch. Remove the croquettes with a wire strainer or slotted spoon and drain on paper towels.

Meanwhile, for the sauce, combine the coconut milk, sugar, and salt in a small saucepan over medium-high heat and bring to a boil. Cook, stirring, until the sugar dissolves, about 1 minute.

Serve the croquettes hot with the dipping sauce.

MAKES 12 CROQUETTES

Almond Milk

This warm drink is very popular in Hong Kong and Guangzhou. Don't let the name confuse you; it is a nondairy beverage. We call it "milk" to describe its smooth, creamy texture. The Chinese almonds add the right yin-yang balance to promote good health.

2½ cups Chinese almonds (apricot kernels)

6½ cups water

Four 1-inch chunks rock sugar or 3 tbsp. granulated sugar

In a large bowl, soak the Chinese almonds in the water until the seeds are swollen, at least 4 hours at room temperature or preferably overnight in the refrigerator.

Working in batches, purée the almonds and soaking water in a blender, whirling until the almonds are the texture of fine sand. Line a colander with a double layer of cheesecloth and set over a clean bowl. Pour the almond purée into the cheesecloth. Gather the corners of the cheesecloth together and gently squeeze out the remaining liquid.

Transfer the almond "milk" to a 2-quart saucepan. Add the sugar and gently cook over medium-low heat, stirring occasionally, until the sugar dissolves. Do not boil the milk.

Ladle into warmed coffee mugs or bowls and serve warm.

MAKES 4 SERVINGS

A NUTTY CONTROVERSY

When is an almond not a nut? When it's a Chinese almond. It may seem nutty, but the Chinese almond is not a nut at all. It's the seed of an apricot native to China.

It has a strong flavor and is a common ingredient in traditional remedies for cold relief. In its raw form, it's actually toxic. The toxicity vanishes once these seeds are heat-processed. For this reason, Chinese almonds are blanched before being sold.

STOP WHINING . . .
YOU CAN DRINK WINE WITH
CHINESE FOOD

After dining at your local Chinese restaurant,
you may think that we're all teetotalers.
But the Chinese have been distilling and
drinking alcohol for thousands of years. Spirits,
especially wine, play an important part
in Chinese celebrations.

In Shanxi Province, I visited the Fenjiu
Distillery, where they make *fenjiu*, China's most
popular rice wine. Here, they bury wine to age
slowly underground. For a private tasting,
Wine-Master Jen unearthed a wine urn that
had been buried some fifty years ago.
He explained that "antique" wine has a better
aroma and is more delicate and intricate
in taste. It was amazing!

In Dali, the Bai people feted me with a plum
banquet and served potent, home-brewed
plum wine, made with plums from trees that had
lived through 400 years of Chinese history.

During the Musuo people's Round Mountain
Festival at Lugu Lake, they toasted nature many
times. Perched on a rock, slightly off balance,
while being filmed, I leaned over to ask my
hosts what they called their local brew.
"Fall-down wine," they announced. And just
then, to their great amusement, I lost
my balance and toppled over!

Chinese Sweet Iced Tea

Chrysanthemum is one of China's most popular tea flowers. These tiny buds are added to strong-flavored teas, or simply in hot water to create an aromatic drink, Chinese tea lovers enjoy the subtle taste of this wonder of nature. Its cooling properties are said to decrease body heat and fever and soothe sore throats.

4 cups water

2 tbsp. chrysanthemum tea

3 teabags oolong tea

Three 1-inch chunks rock sugar or 4 tbsp. honey

Ice cubes

In a medium saucepan, bring the water to a boil. Add the chrysanthemum and oolong teas, remove from the heat, and let steep for 15 minutes. Strain into a pitcher. Add the sugar, stirring until it dissolves, then refrigerate until ready to serve.

Fill 4 tall, chilled glasses with ice and pour the tea over the ice.

MAKES 4 SERVINGS

Ginger Ale

How's this for deconstructing an American classic? Or did the idea of ginger ale actually originate in China, just as spaghetti did? In any event, use an older, more flavorful ginger for this recipe. The young ones are restless and are best suited for stir-fry dishes.

SYRUP

1 cup sugar

1 cup water

⅓ cup coarsely chopped ginger

1 bottle (2 liters) seltzer water or club soda

Ice cubes

To make the syrup, combine the sugar, water, and ginger together in a 1-quart saucepan. Cook over medium-low heat, stirring occasionally, until the sugar dissolves. Remove from the heat, let cool, and pour through a strainer into a small pitcher, discarding the ginger. Refrigerate until ready to serve.

Fill 8 tall, chilled glasses with ice. Divide the syrup among the glasses. Pour 1 cup of the seltzer into each glass. Serve with a straw.

MAKES 8 SERVINGS

The Art of Tea

Ever notice Chinese friends lightly tapping their fingers as you pour their tea? No, they're not impatiently signaling you to hurry up; they're offering a subtle gesture of thanks. This custom allegedly began when a Ching Dynasty emperor, fond of appearing incognito at public teahouses, poured his manservant's tea. The flustered servant, unable to bow in thanks lest he reveal the emperor's disguise, signaled his obedience by tapping his index and middle fingers on the table, creating a simulated bow.

In China, a teacup is filled not just with a drink, but with significance. Just as people meet over coffee in the West, the Chinese make deals and form friendships over tea. Tea is a way of life, historically tied to the economy. Once a major export item, blocks of tea were even exchanged as currency. China's tea became so prized that it inspired a Western idiom: If someone says they wouldn't do something "for all the tea in China," it means they wouldn't do it no matter how precious the reward.

Ancient Chinese first viewed tea as medicine. Buddhist monks drank tea for meditation; soothing, yet tinged with caffeine, it produced the desired state of calm alertness. In the eighth century, the poet Lu Yu popularized tea drinking by proclaiming that it cleared the mind and inspired new thought. Affluent people and writers began gathering at teahouses for animated discussions and musical entertainment. Tea drinking became common, and tea was eventually listed as one of seven indispensable items for family life.

Today, China produces eight thousand varieties of tea. Regions specialize in different teas just as French regions do with wine. In some tea plantations, centuries-old tea bushes reserved for emperors still bloom! At national tea contests, judges inhale the scents of teas and then slurp them from spoons, letting the complex flavors play on their tongues. This is serious business; winning teas sell for astounding sums.

Some fear that new coffee habits might displace tea. But China's growing middle class is demanding more quality tea. The teahouse remains a respite, even in modern cities. Customs still observed at teahouses date back centuries. People once placed pet crickets in empty teapots. Tea servers occasionally removed lids, poured in tea, and drowned these pets, and so began today's practice of pouring refills only into open-lidded pots. Teacups don't have handles because if the cup is too hot to hold, the tea is thought to be too hot for the body. Yu Lu, in his *Classic of Tea*, advised breathing in tea's essence before savoring the flavor, so tea connoisseurs sniff a cup before sipping one. Connoisseurs are vigilant about every aspect of tea making, even naming the water temperatures to be used for specific teas: "shrimp eyes" means bubbles on the water's edge, "crab eyes" means bubbles rising from below, and "dragon eyes" means a rolling boil.

At modern teahouses you find new art forms inspired by tea. Tea paintings and calligraphy grace the walls, and contemporary "tea music" composed specifically to accompany tea-drinking plays in the background. Fruit and herb flavors infuse teas, and bubble teas, with little tapioca pearls, are a favorite of youngsters.

An exciting culinary innovation involves using tea, in powdered form, fresh, or dried, or tea seed oil in main dishes, soups, marinades, tempura, cakes, and desserts—the possibilities are endless.

Many Chinese attribute their longevity to tea. Although it does contain healthful catechins and antioxidants, I believe tea is good for you because drinking it means taking a rest and spending quality time with friends and family!

Lemongrass Tea with Ginseng

When is your tea worth many times the value of the cup in which it sits? When it is laced with ginseng! Some rare ginseng roots can cost up to $10,000. These days, health experts are studying ginseng's health benefits, including enhanced energy—what we call "chi" in China. The next time you propose a toast to good health, do it with ginseng tea.

8 stalks lemongrass

2 pods cardamom, lightly crushed

2 whole star anise

1 cinnamon stick

Three 1-inch chunks rock sugar or 2 tbsp. granulated sugar

6 cups cold water

4 teabags green tea

3 teabags instant ginseng tea

Using the flat side of a large knife, bruise 2 of the lemongrass stalks.

In a 2-quart saucepan, combine the 2 bruised lemongrass stalks, the cardamom, star anise, cinnamon, sugar, and water and bring to a boil over high heat. Reduce the heat to medium-low and simmer gently for 10 minutes. Remove from the heat, add the teabags, and let steep for 10 minutes.

Strain the tea into a 2-quart pitcher, discarding the solids, and refrigerate until ready to serve.

Fill 6 tall, chilled glasses with ice and pour the tea over the ice. Garnish each with one of the remaining lemongrass stalks.

MAKES 6 SERVINGS

Li Hing Mui Lemon Drop

Salty plums are a very popular snack in Southern China. In powdered form, known as *li hing mui*, salty plum enhances food and drinks by adding a combination of salty and sweet flavors. This drink is very concentrated, which makes it an interesting agent to add to a variety of fruit juices. The spice goes well with all types of food, though it's best on fruit, candy, and the rims of cocktail glasses.

RIM GARNISH

1 tbsp. granulated sugar

1 tbsp. *li hing mui* powder

1 cup ice

1 cup vodka

⅓ cup superfine sugar

¼ cup freshly squeezed lemon juice

1 tbsp. *li hing mui* powder

2 slices lemon for garnish

To make the rim garnish, combine the granulated sugar and 1 tsp. *li hing mui* powder in a wide, shallow bowl. Fill another wide, shallow bowl with water. Dip the rims of 2 martini glasses into the water. Dip the wet rims into the rim garnish.

To make the cocktail, fill a cocktail shaker with the ice. Add the vodka, superfine sugar, lemon juice, and *li hing mui* powder; cover and shake until the sugar dissolves. Divide the cocktail between the 2 prepared glasses. Garnish each with a slice of lemon.

MAKES 2 SERVINGS

ONLINE RESOURCES

·····································

Chef Martin Yan's Culinary Arts Center (CAC)

Looking for a gourmet adventure program to China? It has always been my dream to create a platform for culinary professionals and home cooks to learn about Chinese and Pan-Asian cuisine while being introduced to the culture. Find out more about how you can join us on a culinary and cultural adventure. **WWW.MYCIC.BIZ**

Circulon Cookware

Circulon, created by Meyer Corporation, is the original hard-anodized nonstick cookware. I use their sturdy, innovative new designs in my home kitchen. **WWW.CIRCULON.COM**

GE Monogram

I am the envy of everyone on the block because of my state-of-the-art kitchen appliances. Learn more about GE Monogram kitchens site. **WWW.MONOGRAM.COM**

Lee Kum Kee Sauces

Bottled and prepackaged sauces will save you time and energy. Lee Kum Kee is a reliable brand used by most Chinese chefs and home cooks. **WWW.LKK.COM**

Master Grade Knife Sharpeners

A sharp knife is a safe knife! If you're looking for an electric knife sharpener, Master Grade is a cut above. WWW.MASTERGRADEKNIFESHARPENER.COM

Melissa's World Variety Produce

Melissa's is a great source for Asian produce and specialty items. You'll find excellent descriptions and pictures of even the most exotic vegetables and tips on how to use and prepare them. The site carries a wide selection of vegetables and fruits from all cuisines. WWW.MELISSAS.COM

Sanyo Home Appliances

Sanyo has been a reliable friend in my kitchen for years. Take a look at their rice cookers, toasters, grills, and more. WWW.SANYO.COM

Tai Foong

Tai Foong's extensive variety of seafood and ready-to-eat products are great when you're in a hurry. WWW.TAIFOONG.COM

MENU SUGGESTIONS

·······································

BANQUET DINNER
Shrimp Tulips (page 86)
Lamb Siu Mai with Spicy Tomato Sauce (page 91)
Jade Lobster (page 168)
Dragon and Lion Head Meatballs (page 197)
Twice-Cooked Duck (page 184)
Five-Spice Flourless Chocolate Cake (page 206)

HOME-STYLE MEAL
Poached Eggplant with SpicyPeanut Sauce (page 71)
Fortune Noodle Meatball Soup (page 98)
Panda's Favorite (page 182)
Carrot Rice (page 123)
Ginger-Garlic Baby Bok Choy (page 106)

QUICK AND EASY
Steamed Tofu with Black Bean Sauce (page 110)
Shangri-la Beef (page 192)
Pan-Fried Noodle Cakes (page 137)
Mango Purée with Coconut Milk (page 204)

MARTIN YAN'S FAVORITES
Golden Curry Pumpkin Soup (page 96)
Preserved Duck with Clay Pot Rice (page 124)
Prosperity Steamed Fish (page 152)
Curry Crab (page 164)

VEGETARIAN
Mushroom Medley Soup (page 93)
Rainbow Stir-Fry (page 116)
Vegetarian Fried Brown Rice (page 127)
Pea Shoots with Soft Tofu (page 112)

PICNIC PERFECT MEAL
Green Salad with Sweet Plum Vinaigrette (page 54)
Yellow Chive Omelet (page 107)
Char Siu with Spicy Pickled Cucumbers (page 172)
Wine-Poached Chicken (page 199)
Chinese Sweet Iced Tea (page 220)

BACKYARD BARBECUE
Sweet Vinegar Peanuts (page 82)
Pickled Vegetables (page 63)
Tea-Infused Chicken Kebabs (page 85)
Grilled Spiced Pork Chops (page 177)
Noodle Salad with Peanut Dressing (page 141)
Lychee Pudding with Strawberry Sauce (page 210)

ACKNOWLEDGMENTS

· ·

The generous support of our sponsors made this television show and companion book possible. Once again, GE Monogram supplied our sleek, well-designed kitchen appliances, enabling us to prepare 10 to 12 dishes a day. Randall Fong, John Schmitt, and the folks at GE are true professionals. I also must thank my friends with GE Monogram for introducing me to the Albert Lee Appliance folks in Seattle and the friendly, helpful staff, who let us turn their store into our studio. Special thanks go to Kelly McMeekin of Albert Lee for accommodating our crew. Sanyo joined us this year and provided us with the most impressive, high-tech electric appliances. The rice cookers were prized items of studio filming—everyone in my kitchen crew wanted to take one home! I thank Grace Chow, Eliza Jen, and Sonia Ramirez of Lee Kum Kee for their continued support; I am excited to use the best selection and quality of sauces used by Chinese chefs and home cooks worldwide. Master Grade knife sharpener gave me the sharp edge I needed to cut through ingredients at lightning speed. Thanks to Jack Chen and Judy Oh for their friendship. And what a mess our show would have been without the right pots and pans! Suzanne Howard, Cathleen Mandigo, and Florence Sheffer and Meyer Corporation came to the rescue with their innovative Circulon collection of cookware, which I use at home. The Hernandez family and Nancy Eisman of Melissa's have supported us through the years, providing us with a variety of Asian produce, from the basics to the exotic. Thanks to Davy Lam and Tai Foong for providing us with the freshest seafood available. Our crew had a comfortable stay at the Doubletree Hotel so we could recuperate for the next day's show. We were fortunate to have two of the most talented chefs as guests on our show, Jennifer Cox and Tom Douglas. I want to thank Chris Ivens-Brown and Compass Group for their friendship and support.

We spent more than two months filming on location in China. Liu and Jagen Wang and the World Association of Chinese Cuisine helped us find the best restaurants in the country. Lily Yuan, Shu Qing Jin, Cecily Xiao Chen, Jiang Yang, and Yuan Yuan Wang of China State Council Information introduced us to many hidden areas of China. Qing Suang Kung of China Travel Service graciously arranged our transportation and travel. I am grateful for the warm hospitality of the people I met along the way and for their customs and life stories that inspired this culinary journey. Thanks to Ming Yang in Guilin, Jianping Cao in Yunnan, Paofeng Li in Lijiang, and Koomu Guo of Lugu Lake, we had an inside look at the lifestyles of minority people in China. It truly was an adventure. We ventured into pristine areas of China and were able to capture these amazing stories on film thanks to Phil Kawasoe and Margus Jukkum. Also thanks to Pauline Wong, who really helped us get this show on the road!

When the director says "Action!" it's very misleading. There is actually more action going on behind the scenes than in front of the camera. Our kitchen crew worked nonstop to help prepare the recipes brought to you in this book and in the TV series. Chef Julie Tan diligently set up my kitchen while kitchen manager James Smith and sous-chef A. J. Faung kept the prep coming. Thanks to Judy Lew for lending her expertise and friendship. Our producer, Anne-Sophie Brieger, kept us organized and on schedule, and executive producer Nat Katzman orchestrated the crew and schedule brilliantly. Director Jim

Killenbeck had the difficult job of capturing everything on camera. My good friends Chef Wai and Chef Yao lent their skill and knowledge in our classic Chinese dishes. And just because filming is over doesn't mean the show is done. Our postproduction editors, Colm Caffrey and Brent Pate, had the daunting task of editing the shows.

Of course, this book would not have been possible without the long hours put in by the Yan Can Cook team. I am grateful to my culinary team for assisting me in fine-tuning these recipes—the sweat and toil of Irene Yim, Julia Lee, and Ken Kao. Thanks to the dedication of Ivan Lai, Elizabeth Reis, and Damon Barham, who help me put my words down on paper. Tara Lee kept everyone on task to meet our cookbook deadlines and to help bring it all together, and Leslie Co and Peter Louie and their research and organization kept us on task. Stephanie Jan goes above and beyond the call of duty. Her versatility has made her an essential member of the Yan Can Cook family. I admire her ability to truly capture our experiences on camera; just look at all the travel photos and you will be impressed. Lastly, I am most grateful to Sue, for her patience and warmth, and for being the yin to my Yan.

Martin Yan's China is about discovering something beyond what you know. Whether you are a Chinese master chef or a home cook who has never touched a wok, I hope this book gives you the inspiration to explore something new, as my friends, colleagues, and family have inspired me.

INDEX

····················

TABLE OF EQUIVALENTS

The exact equivalents in the following tables have been rounded for convenience.

Liquid / Dry Measures

U.S.	METRIC
¼ teaspoon	1.25 milliliters
½ teaspoon	2.5 milliliters
1 teaspoon	5 milliliters
1 tablespoon (3 teaspoons)	15 milliliters
1 fluid ounce (2 tablespoons)	30 milliliters
¼ cup	60 milliliters
⅓ cup	80 milliliters
½ cup	120 milliliters
1 cup	240 milliliters
1 pint (2 cups)	480 milliliters
1 quart (4 cups; 32 ounces)	960 milliliters
1 gallon (4 quarts)	3.84 liters
1 ounce (by weight)	28 grams
1 pound	454 grams
2.2 pounds	1 kilogram

Oven Temperatures

FAHRENHEIT	CELSIUS	GAS
250	120	½
275	140	1
300	150	2
325	160	3
350	180	4
375	190	5
400	200	6
425	220	7
450	230	8
475	240	9
500	260	10

Lengths

U.S.	METRIC
⅛ inch	3 millimeters
¼ inch	6 millimeters
½ inch	12 millimeters
1 inch	2.5 centimeters